Book 1

A Logical Approach to Spelling

Highly structured curriculum on the sounds in words and the application of spelling rules.

Jurina Dean

Thank you

I want to express my gratitude to Maiya for introducing us to this amazing journey. If it weren't for your unique way of learning, many wouldn't have the benefit of this book. A big thank you to Giulia and Jemimah for bringing this book to life with your contributions. Manu, you created such an adorable character for the book—thank you! And lastly, to my husband, who patiently listened to hours of my progress updates. Love you so much!

Index

Preface

Welcome to the journey of helping your child learn to read and write in English! I invite you to pause and take a moment to explore this preface, as it sets the stage for the incredible impact this book can have on your child's learning experience.

As a mother of four living in Geneva, Switzerland, I understand the unique challenges and opportunities that come with raising children in a multi language environment. My eldest daughter breezed through her weekly spelling lists, effortlessly mastering each word. However, my second daughter faced a different path. The frustration she experienced with her spelling lists was palpable. While she could learn words, recalling them a week later felt like an insurmountable task.

After discovering that she had dyslexia and short-term verbal memory challenges, I embarked on a five-year journey of learning and discovering how to work through the curriculum with an alternative method.

I was advised to focus on the 300 most frequently used words in English. We dedicated a year to mastering these words, achieving a 50% success rate. While this was a start, I knew there had to be a better way. My daughter excelled in math, successfully following logical steps to solve problems. This inspired me to research a logical approach to spelling.

In my quest to find effective resources, I explored many different books and countless online materials. I realised that a vast amount of these resources lacked the structure and repetition necessary for lasting retention.

While I couldn't find a single definitive resource, I began piecing together a beautiful method for learning to spell in English—one that emphasises a logical structure, much like math. This book aims to provide that framework.

In English spelling, we often encounter exceptions to the rule, but we'll tackle these later in our journey. Initially, we focus on what makes sense phonetically and explore homophones as a key theme throughout this book. Together, we'll play detective, investigating the fascinating world of different spellings. As a child's brain develops, they will naturally anchor these "exception to the rule" words through their growing photographic memory.

Our curriculum provides a strong foundation and support for visual memory and logical thinking, transitioning to reliance on photographic memory as your child progresses. We cover all spelling elements of national curriculums, but with a difference – we emphasise the sounds in words and foster confidence in blending simple words for future success.

We'll explore "borrowed" words from other languages, highlighting the similarities that can serve as helpful anchors. Towards the end of the series, we'll address words that often cause confusion early on for children who find spelling challenging. These words will align correctly in your child's mind as they mature, so we won't focus on teaching them prematurely. Instead, we'll nurture their spelling confidence in stages of mind-readiness.

At the end of each section, you'll find a word bank. Use this to create spelling tests until your child masters each word, revisiting it throughout the series. Be mindful of your child's attention span, and keep lessons between 10 to 30 minutes a day. Consistent, short repetitions are key! Help them understand why words are spelled a certain way, and revisit the word bank after a month, and again after three months.

You are making a wonderful difference in your child's learning journey! Enjoy every moment of this experience—it truly passes quickly. Happy learning together!

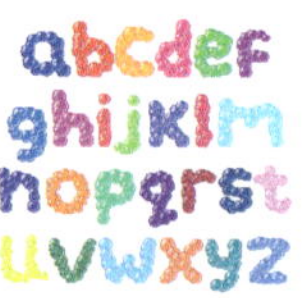

Tips

It's important to take things step by step! First, let's focus on mastering the sounds of the alphabet before introducing their names. This will help build a strong foundation for blending sounds as we read and write. Once your child is confident with the sounds, we can gently introduce the five vowel names (like a for acorn). Remember, knowing the ABC song isn't necessary for learning to read or write the first words (CVC words); understanding the sound each letter makes is key.

As we progress, let's ensure your child is comfortable with small letters before moving on to capital letters. Capital letters are special and are mainly used for names and at the beginning of sentences.

When it comes to print and cursive letters, let's take our time! Mastering print letters first will help avoid confusion, especially with letters like b and d.

Happy spelling!
Jurina Dean

What a typical week with this book looks like

Daily practice in reading, writing, and spelling is essential, and it should be fun! Pay attention to your child's focus and adjust as needed. Think of their attention span as a muscle that we're gradually strengthening. We can create a consistent structure for lessons or mix things up based on your child's energy and mood. On some days, starting with a spelling test followed by new activities can work well. Reading should ideally be a separate session, especially if it's longer than five minutes. Let's keep lessons short—no more than 20 minutes without reading.

Make sure to celebrate each achievement, no matter how small! Remember, the key is to review concepts regularly and keep the learning experience joyful.

To summarise

- Learning a concept once a week, reviewing it daily
- Spelling test 5-10 words (To succeed, you have to write short spelling tests at least twice a week.)
- Exercises
- Forming a few letters
- Reading 5-20 mins a day

Levels of mastering reading and spelling

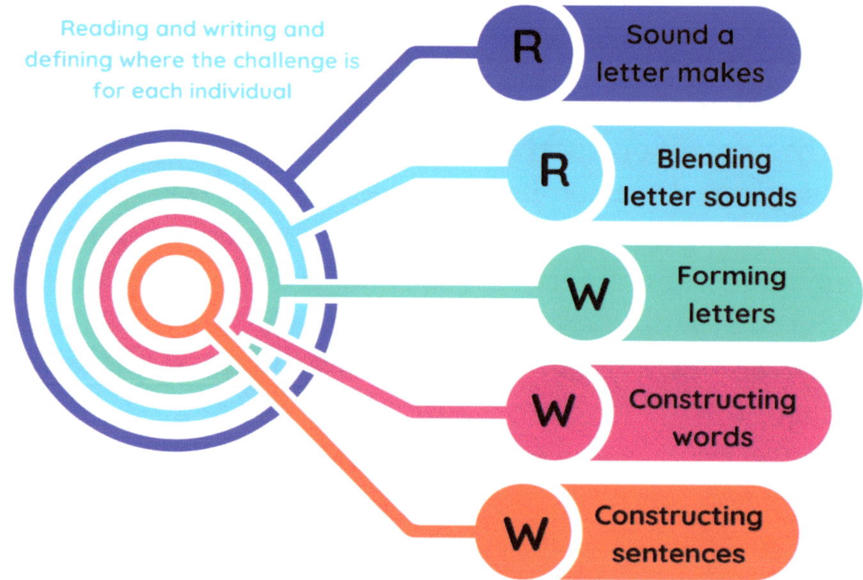

If your ever find an exercise to be a bit challenging, don't worry! You can make it easier by simplifying one of the skills involved. For instance, writing a sentence utilizes all the skills mentioned above, but by using words that are already written down, you can focus on one skill at a time while still learning, creating, and building your confidence.

This approach can also be applied to word-building. If you use letters that are already formed on paper, you can create words more easily. By "stripping out" some of the complexities of a task, you can help identify specific areas that may need extra attention.

It's important to remember that every child is unique in the way they learn. Some may find blending words to be a bit tricky, while they might excel at forming letters, and vice versa. Likewise, some children may be able to construct a sentence beautifully in conversation but may need more support when it comes to writing it down.

By teaching from multiple strength points, we can truly enhance the development of each individual child. Together, we can create a supportive learning environment that encourages growth and confidence!

Reading and spelling

Each child will have their own unique way of mastering reading, writing, and spelling. That's perfectly okay! We'll spend plenty of time exploring CVC (consonant+vowel+consonant=cat) words and longer consonant-blended words. While this stage may feel a bit repetitive at times, it's important to take your time and enjoy the process. Building a solid foundation now will make future learning smoother and boost confidence along the way.

As we progress, we'll wrap up with sentence building and take a quick look at the double "o" sound and the "qu" sound. Feel free to move through this book at your own pace, revisiting different exercises and practicing those more challenging concepts.

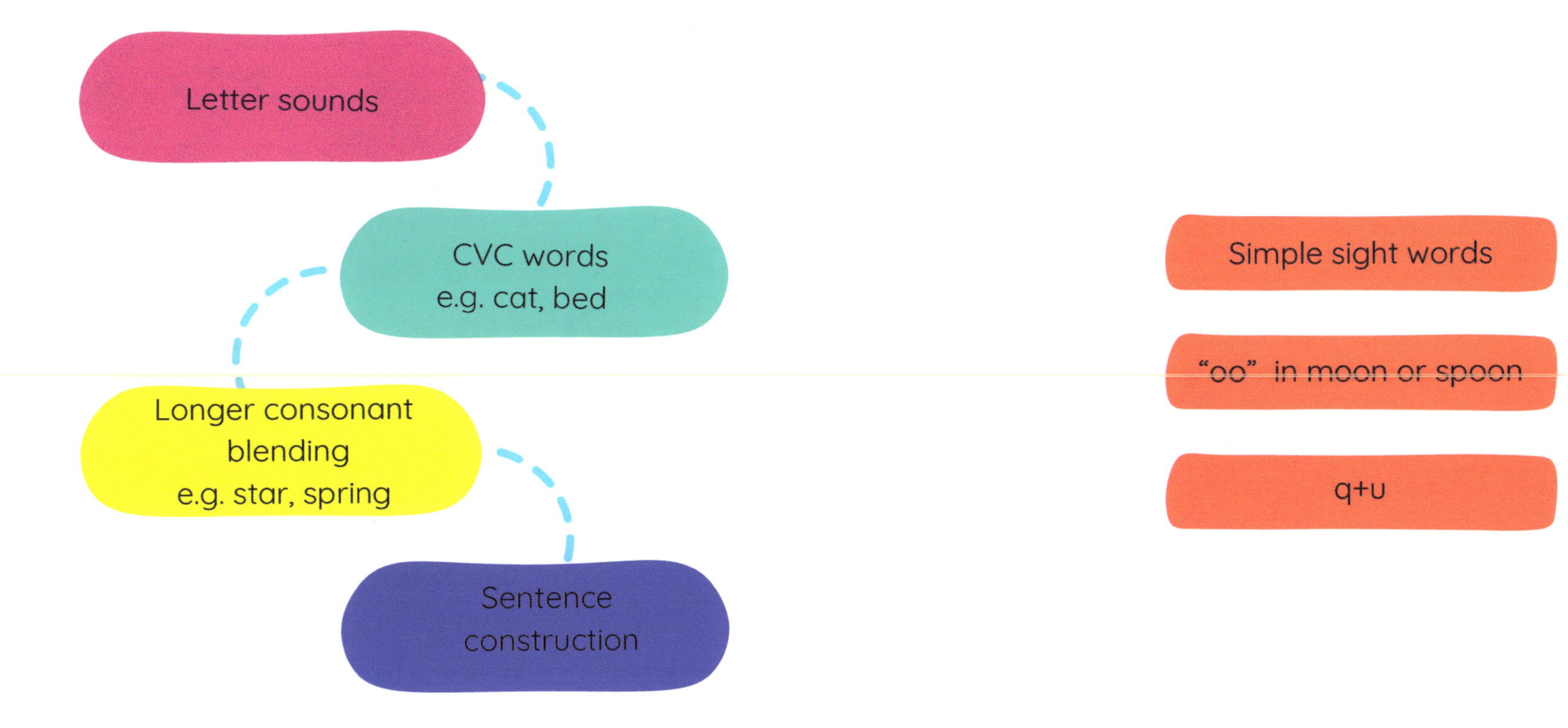

It is important not to say the name of the letter, but the sound it makes! Not "A" for acorn but "a" for apple.

Make sure when forming these letters, that the hand does not lift up when it doesn`t need to. Over-emphasise where to start the letter, that the "t" ends with a tail, the "b" is for boot or "b" for the bat and **then** the ball and "d"for doorknob and **then** the door. This section is very important, together with the sound of the letters. Spelling of words will be easier with these foundations properly established. It will build their confidence when they can make the letters properly.

Trace the whole letter. Start at the green dot. Finish at the red dot. You cannot lift up your hand until you have made the whole letter and you reached a red dot.

If your child has only done two letters and is finding it frustrating, do not ask them to do a whole row. With a lot of encouragement, ask them to do only one more letter, and talk them through that letter being formed.

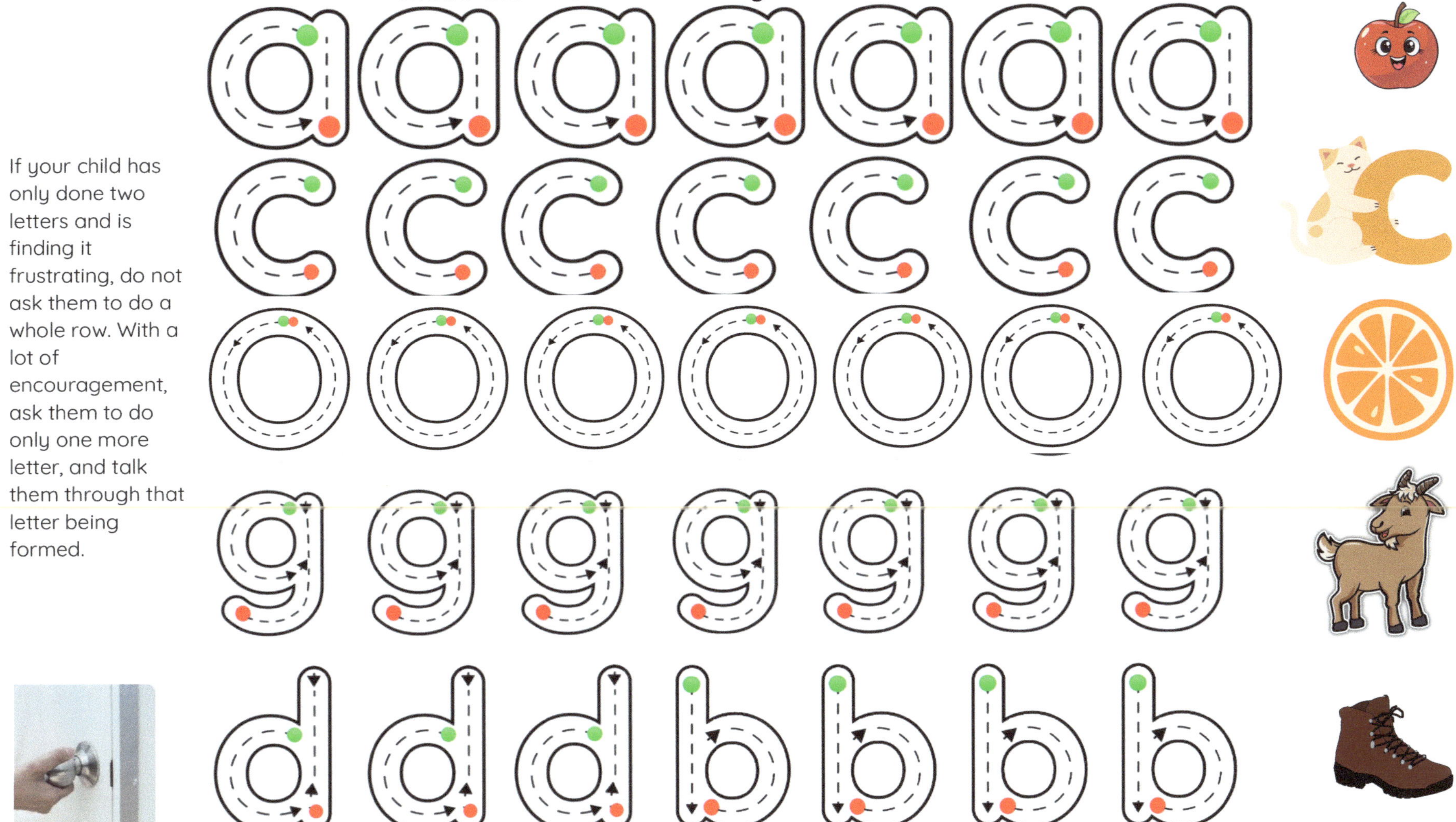

Practise your letters a few more times.

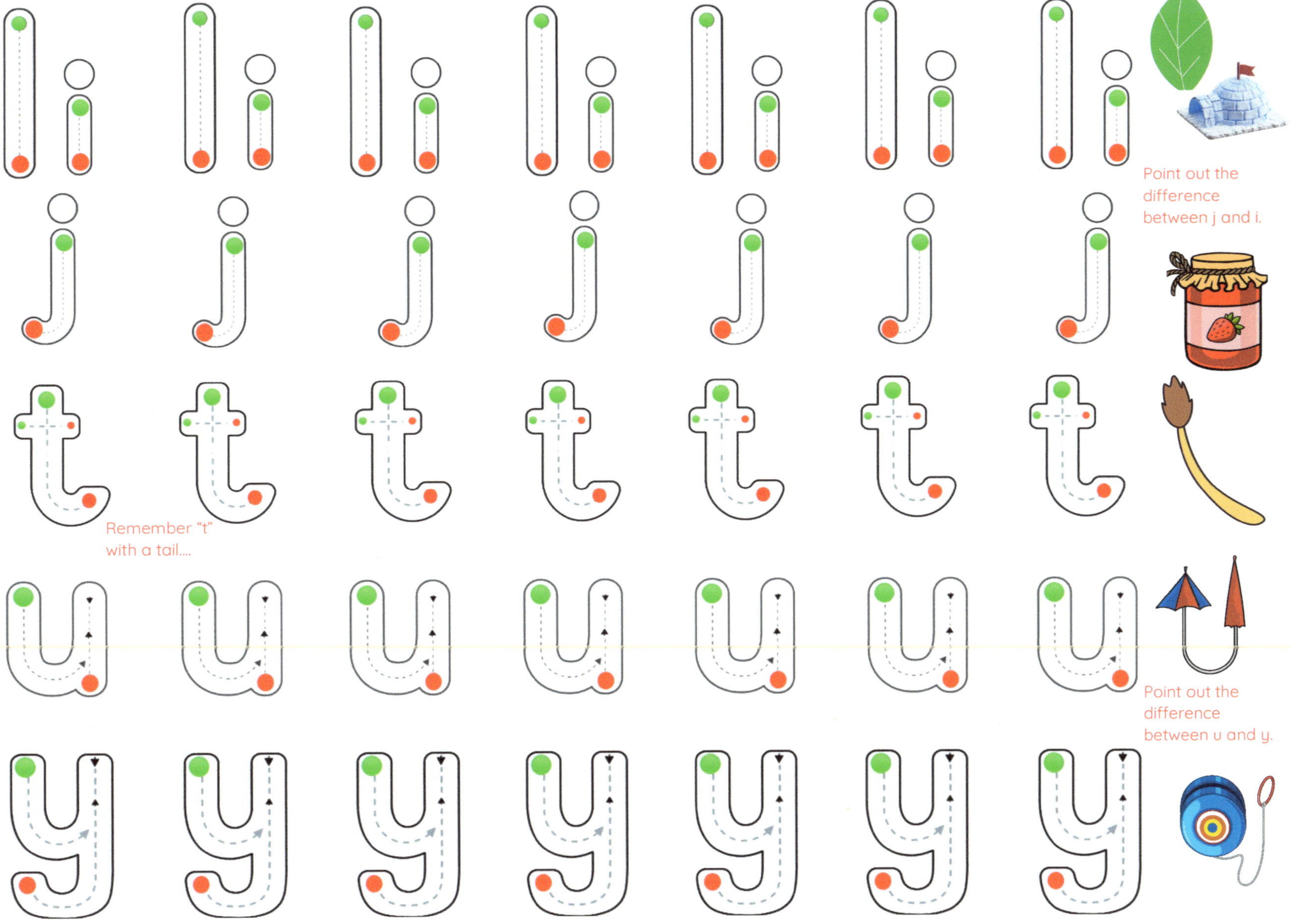
Point out the difference between j and i.
Remember "t" with a tail....
Point out the difference between u and y.

l i l i l i l i

j j j j

t t t t

u u u u

y y y y

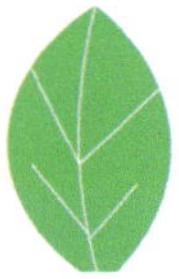

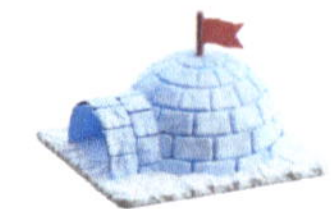

Practise your letters a few more times.

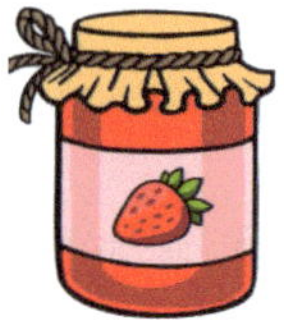

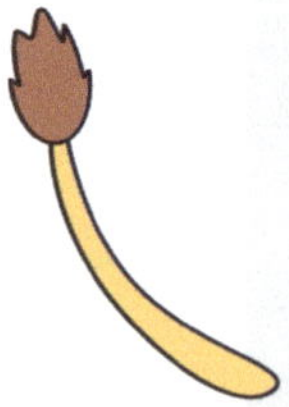

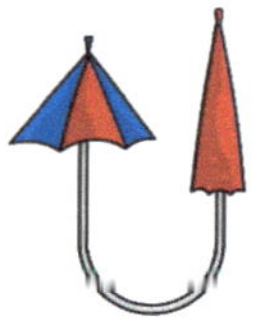

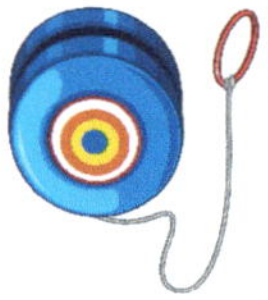

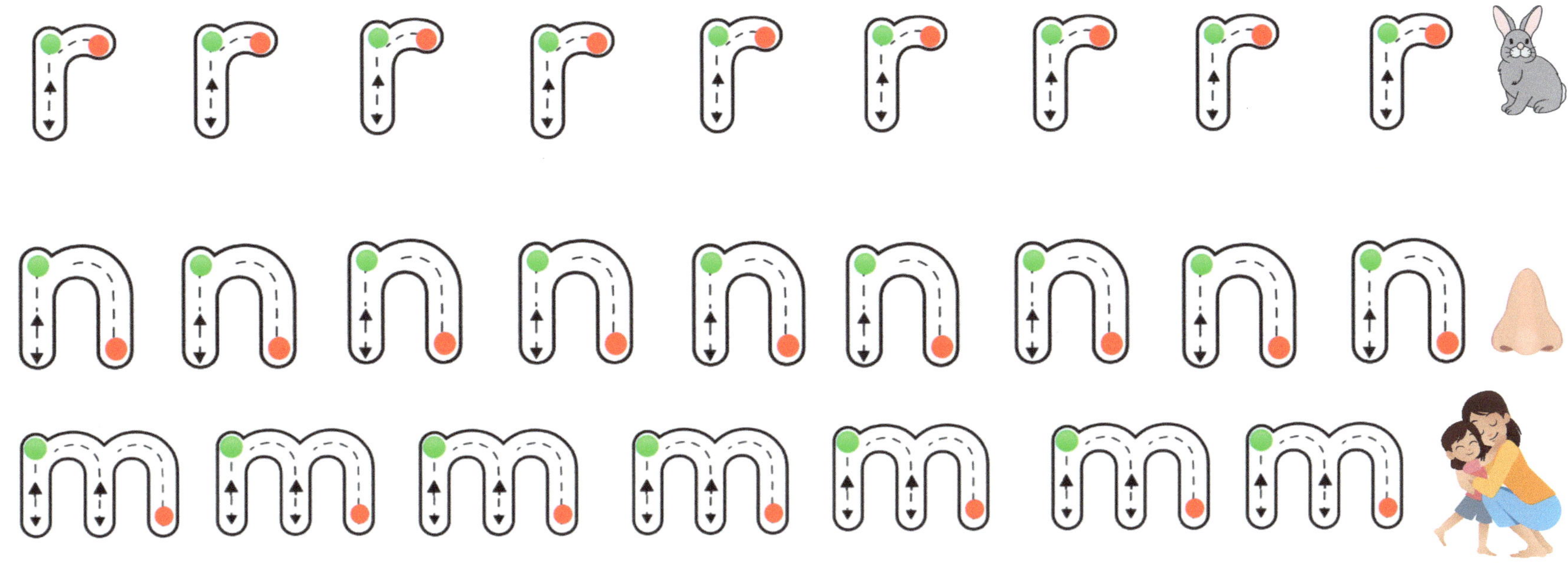

When confusion starts to creep in with the introduction or awareness of capital letters, look together at the differences. Use lined paper to work together on the differences between capital and small letters.

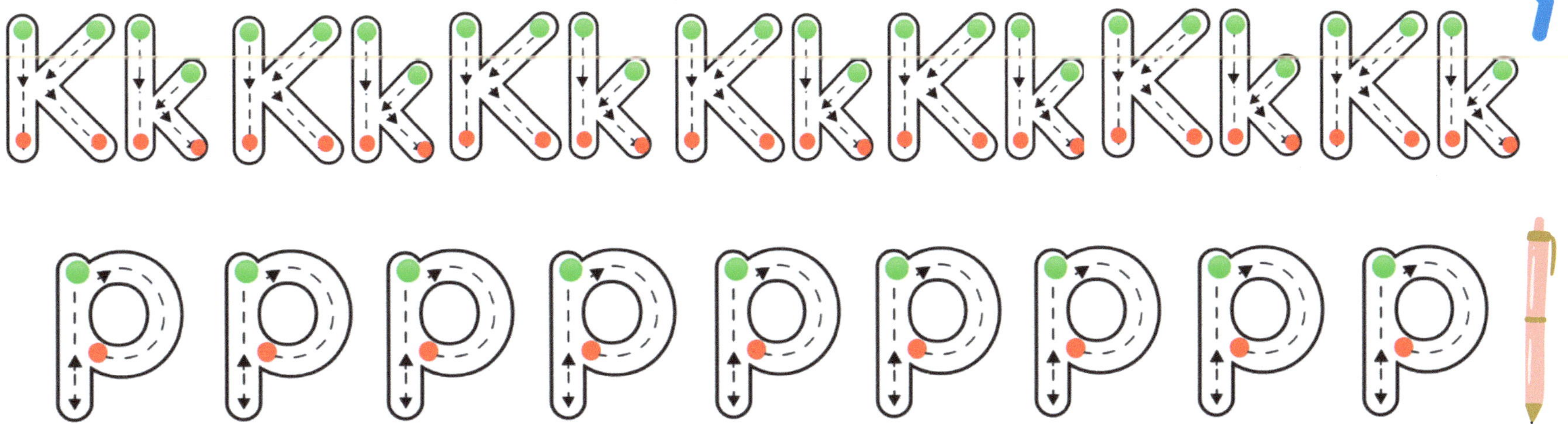

r r r r

n n n n

m m m m

Kk Kk Kk

p p p p

Practise your letters a few more times.

e e e e e e e

s s s s s s s

z z z z z z z

Look at the letter z and the number 2 together. They are very similar and it will help in not forming these the wrong way round.

2 2 2 2 2 2 2

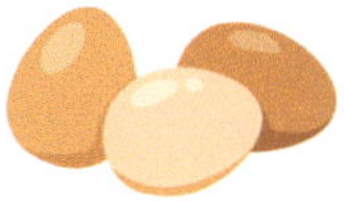

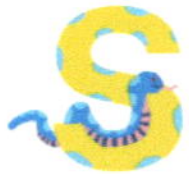

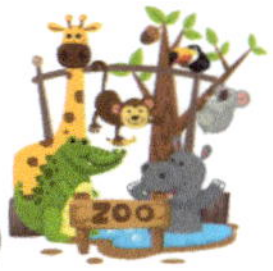

After each letter below is formed, asked them which one is which. Remember "q" is for quick and "p" is for pen.

q p q p q p q

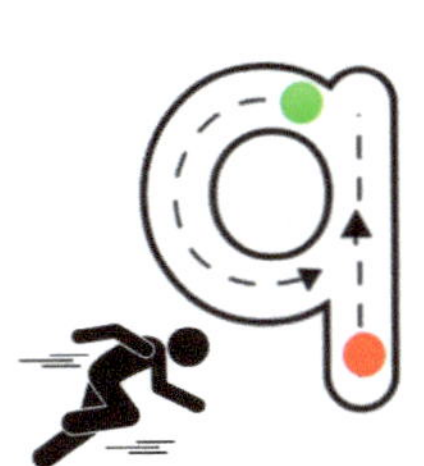

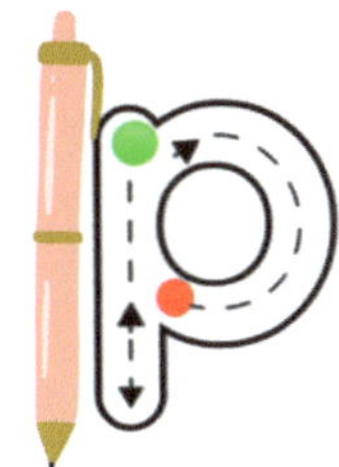

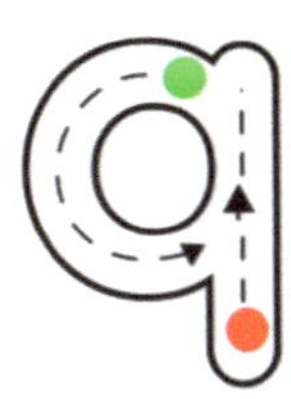

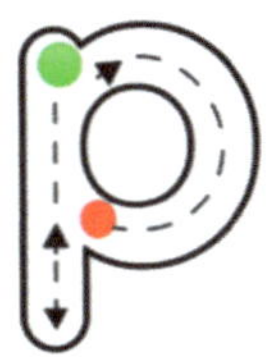

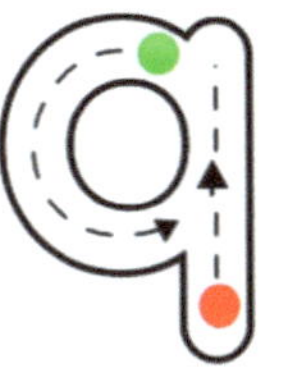

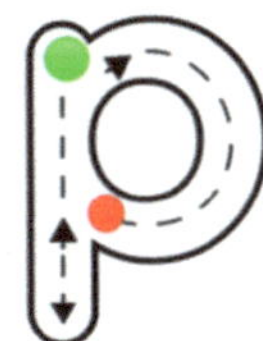

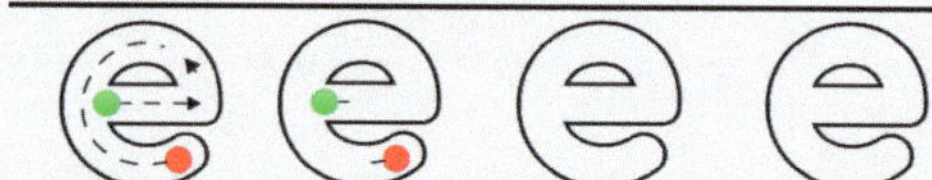

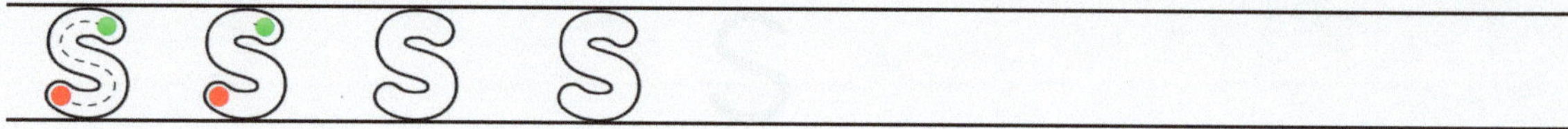

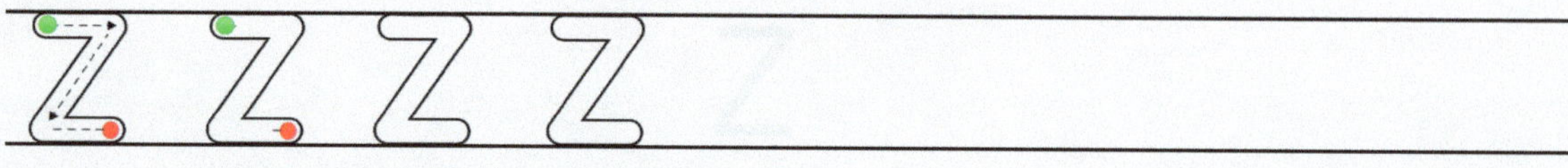

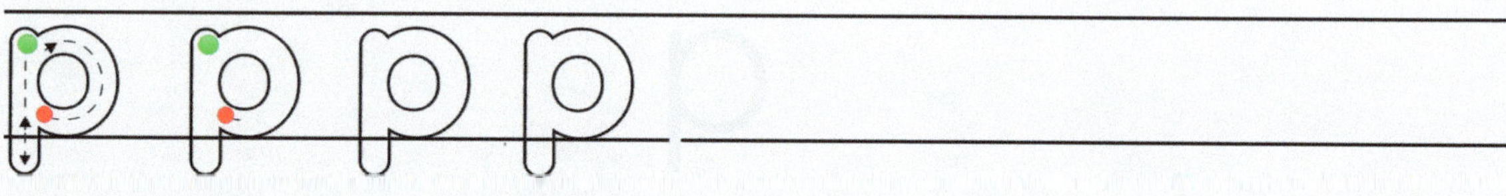

Practise your letters a few more times.

hn hn hn hn hn hn
Remember "w" is for whale and "v" is for van.
wv wv wv w wv wv wv
f f f f f f f
"f" we make by going from top to bottom, and then from left to right.
x x x x x x x

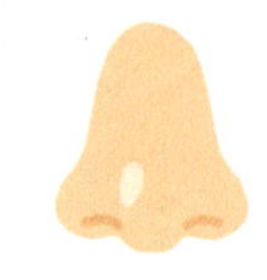

Practise your letters a few more times.

Practise the letters you find most challenging here!

Write more 6 and 9 numbers on this page.

Say this over and over again: 6 and 9 both starts at the **top**. 9 with his tummy first and then ending at the bottom. He is older and can stand on one leg.

It is important not to say the name of the letter, but the sound it makes!

Connect only the pictures that start with the letter in the middle.

ant arrow apple astronaut avocado ostrich octopus orange otter cloud caterpillar cat cow sun snake seven skate tiger tray ten tent tree ill insect igloo

Connect only the pictures that start with the letter in the middle.

egg elephant envelope fox fork frog fig fire fish lamp lion llama leopard honey hen hay hat nose nine nest nurse map meat mouth map

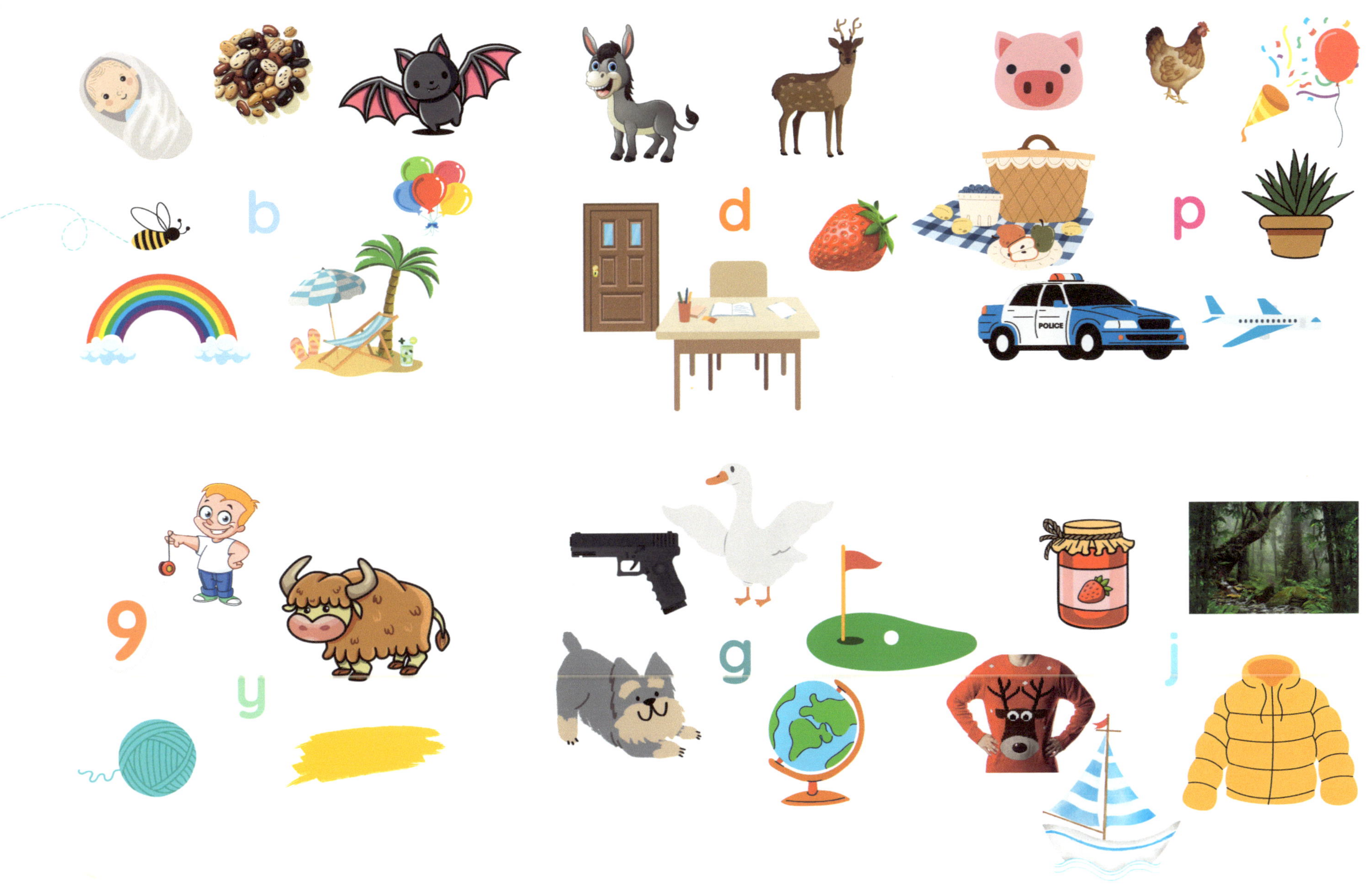

Connect only the pictures that start with the letter in the middle.

baby beans bat balloons beach bee donkey deer desk door pig party plant/pot plane police picnic yo-yo yak yellow yarn gun goose golf globe jam jungle jacket jumper

Connect only the pictures that start with the letter in the middle.

kiss ketchup kettle king queen quick question quack robot rabbit red rat umbrella up underwear vulture van vest vegetables window whale water wind whisk

Circle all the pictures that start with the letter z and right tick the number 2 pictures

What letter does the picture start with? See how many you can connect.

apple boot cat door egg, fan goat horse igloo jam, kangaroo leaf mum nose orange, pool doll ball hat, arrow olives macaroons necklace umbrella, grass jungle ill lamp hamster

What letter does the picture start with? See how many you can connect.

tail pen rabbit quick umbrella snake, van x-ray yo-yo wheel zoo, ant elephant octopus ink umbrella, pig bun donkey guitar, trampoline rainbow key zero, moon underwear/pants numbers rocket

Which letter does the word for each picture starts with?

pie butterfly doctor books grasshopper gold dinosaur dog peg pig donkey gorilla pen bun

Which letter does the word for each picture starts with?

umbrella nose volcano medal necklace van mud vegetables underpants moon nails nun

Circle all the "b" letters. There is one in each group of four.

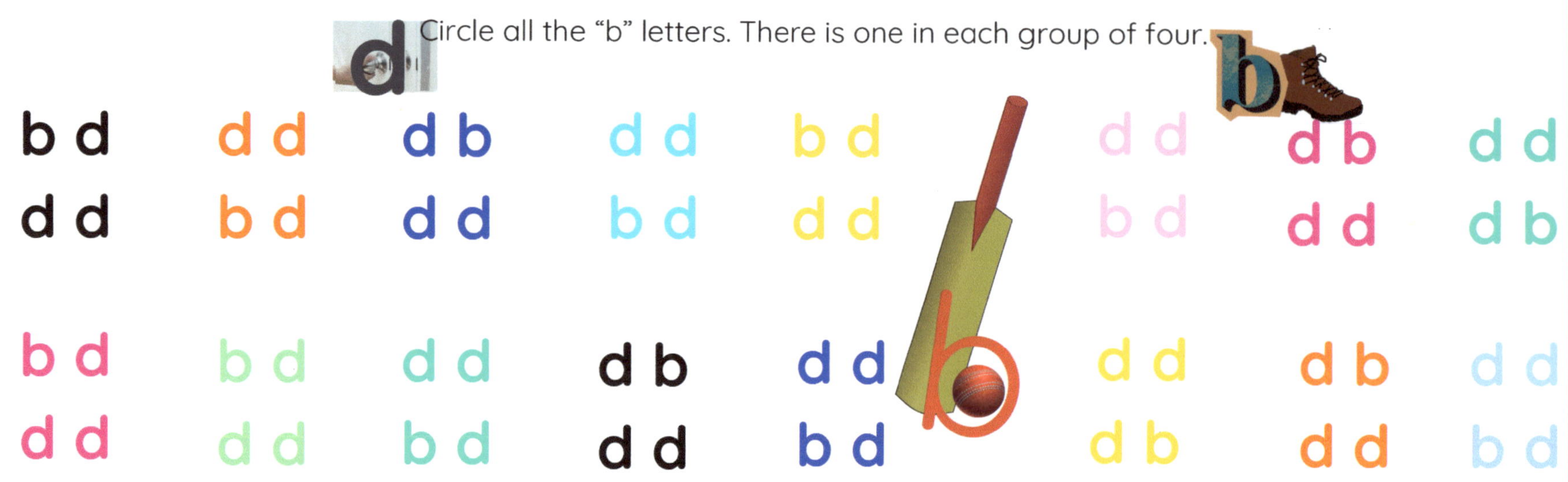

Colour all the "b" letters red

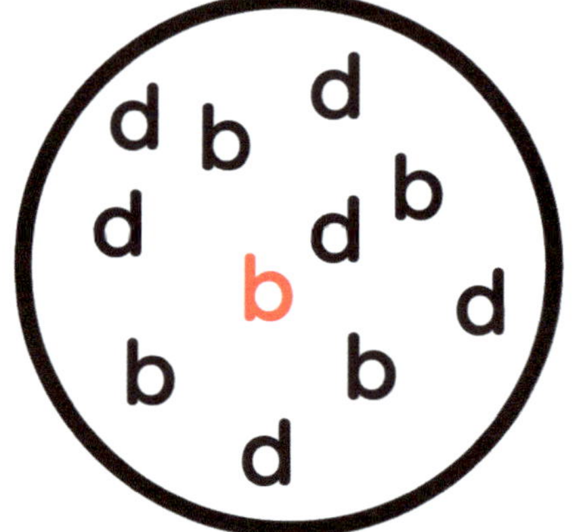

Circle all the "b" letters.

b b b d b b b d d b d b b d d b

Colour all the "d" letters green

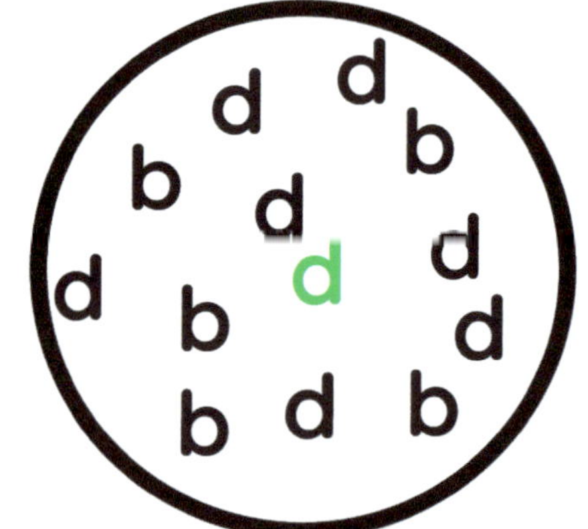

Circle all the "d" letters.

b b b d b b b d d b d b b d d b

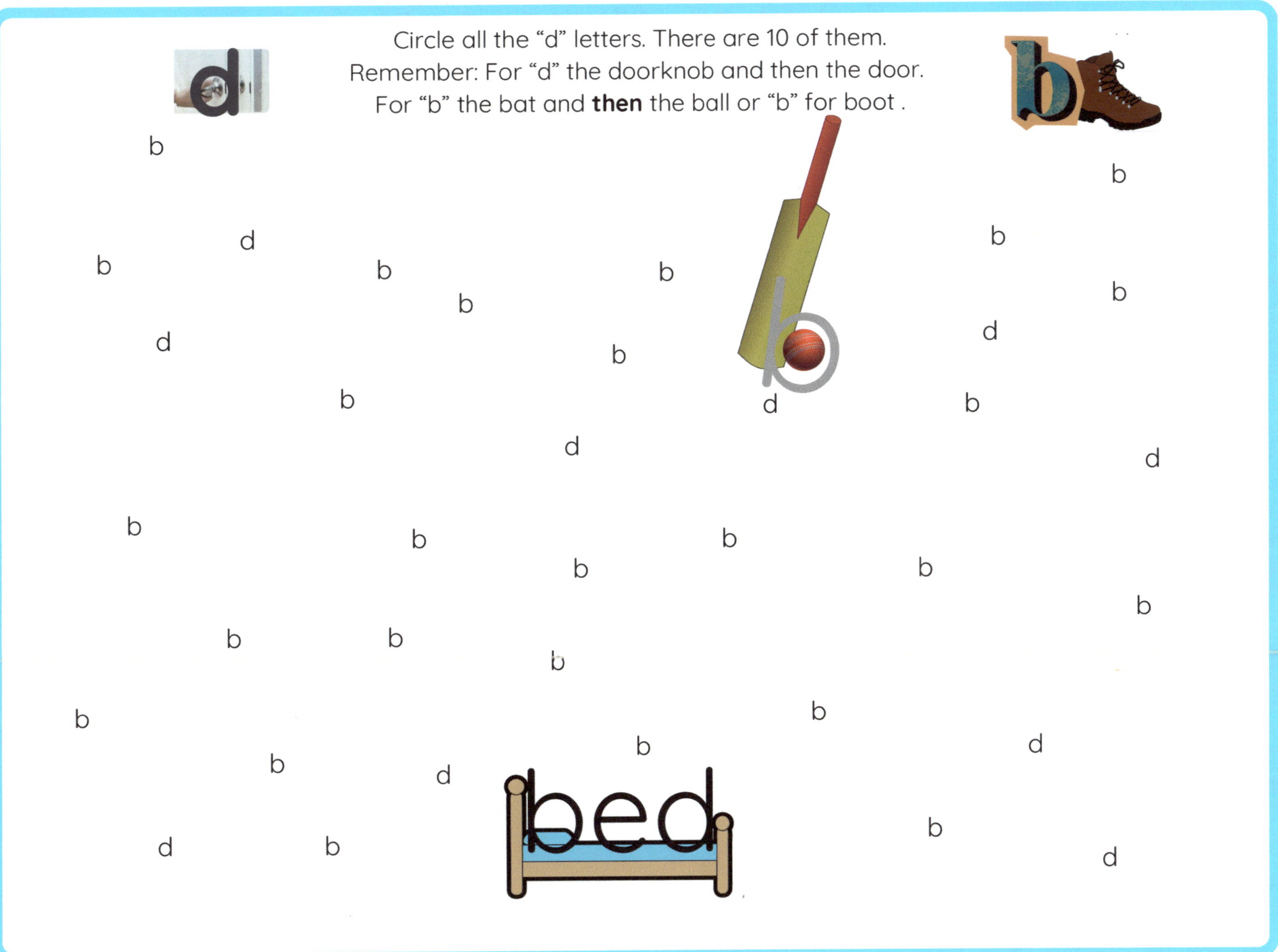
Circle all the "d" letters. There are 10 of them.
Remember: For "d" the doorknob and then the door.
For "b" the bat and **then** the ball or "b" for boot .
bed

Draw a line from the word to the matching picture

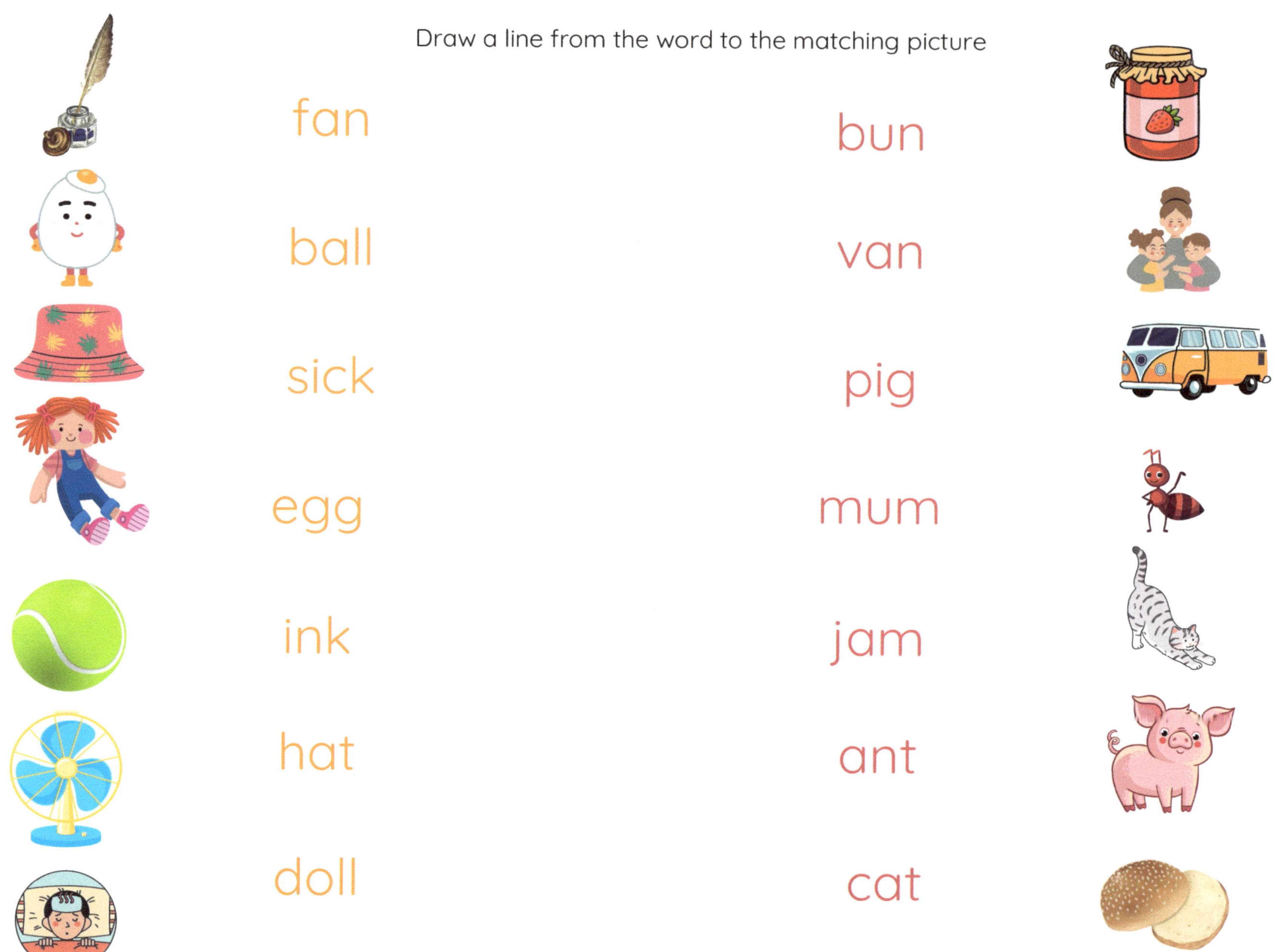

HINT: 1. What letter does the word start with? 2. What letter does the word end with? 3. What letter can you hear in the middle?

Draw a line from the word to the matching picture

cup	bat
bed	rat
bus	hug
fox	nut
mud	cap
dog	bag
sun	log

HINT: 1. What letter does the word start with? 2. What letter does the word end with? 3. What letter can you hear in the middle?

Cut these letters out .
Cover the words on this page .
Build the word by choosing the correct letters.
Check if you are correct.

1. What does the word start with?
2. What letter do you hear at the end?
3. Which of these 5 letters do you hear in the middle: a o u e or i

s	a	t
c	a	t
m	a	t
r	a	t
t	i	n
f	o	x

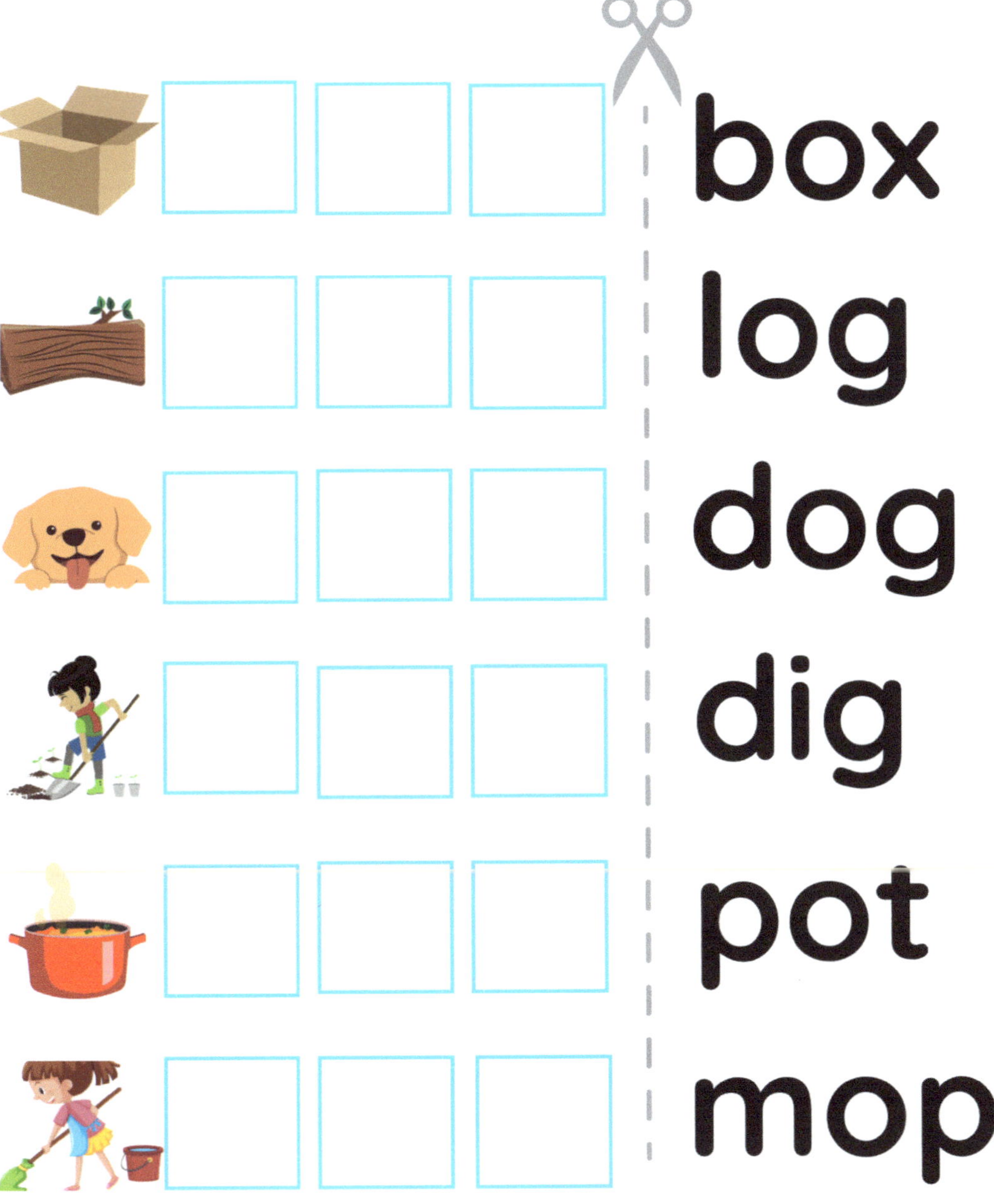

b	o	x
l	o	g
d	o	g
d	i	g
p	o	t
m	o	p

b	e	d
r	e	d
p	e	n
t	e	n
l	e	g
p	e	g

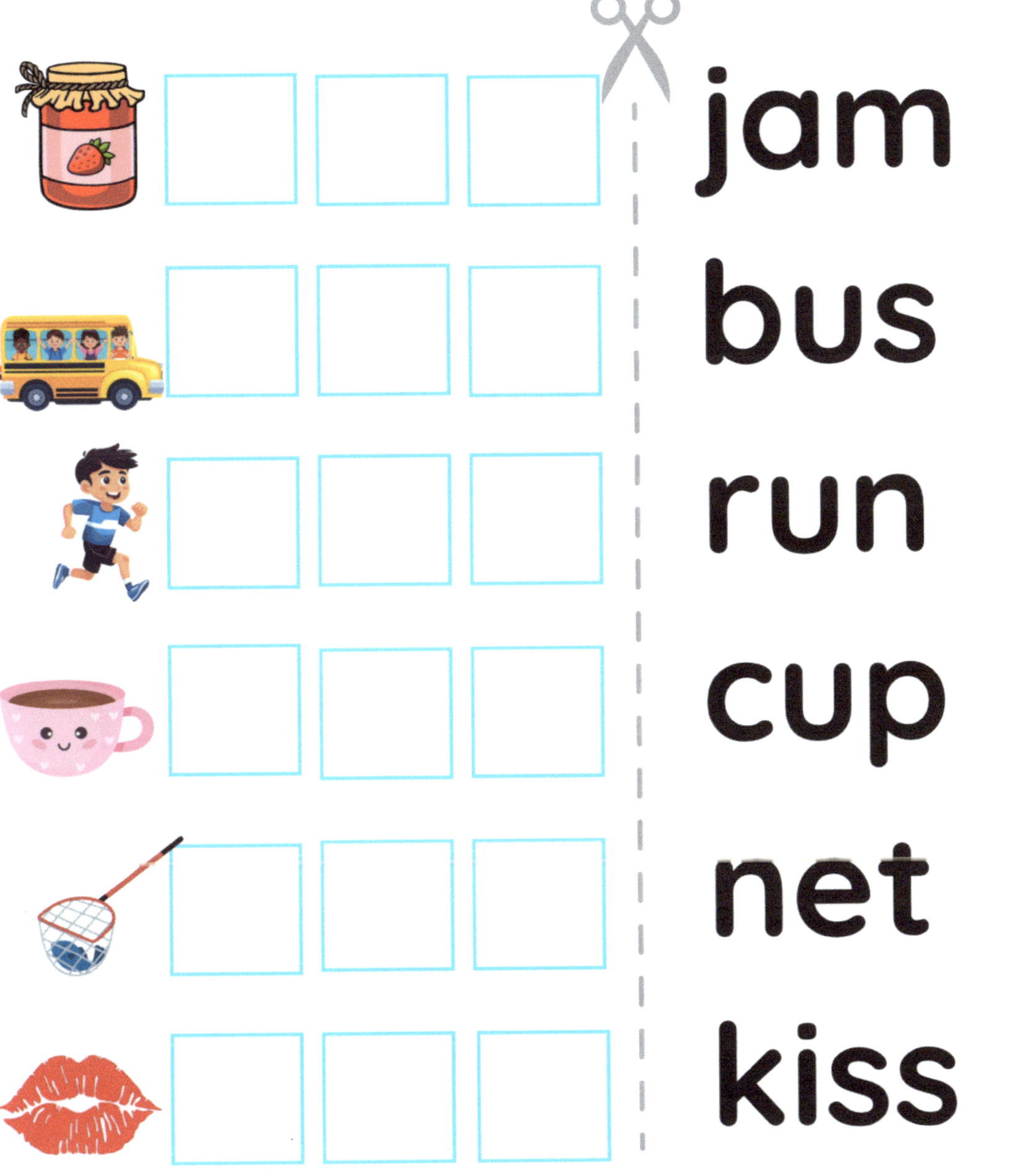

j	a	m
b	u	s
r	u	n
c	u	p
n	e	t
k	i	ss

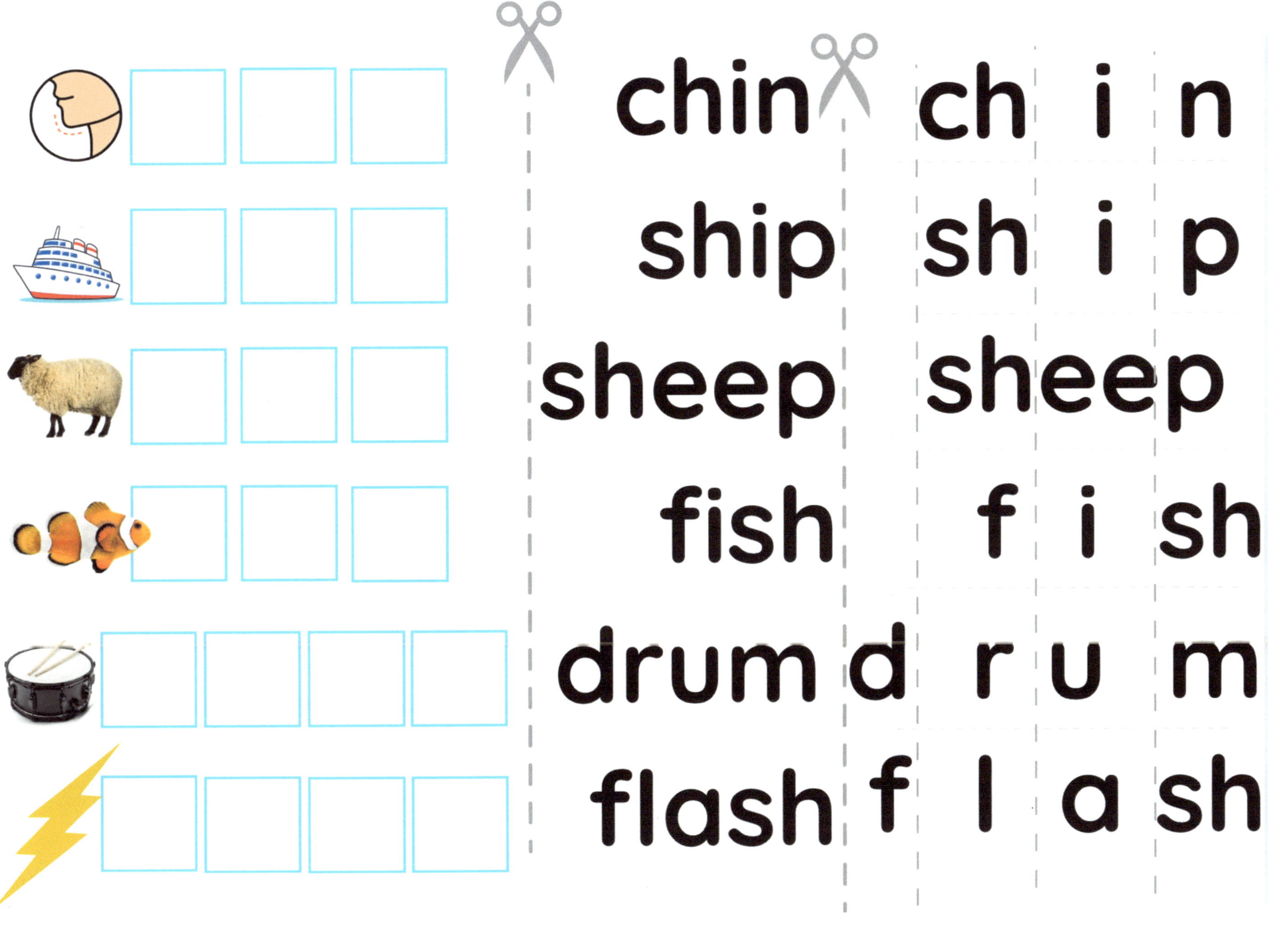
chin
ship
sheep
fish
drum
flash
ch i n
sh i p
sheep
f i sh
d r u m
f l a sh

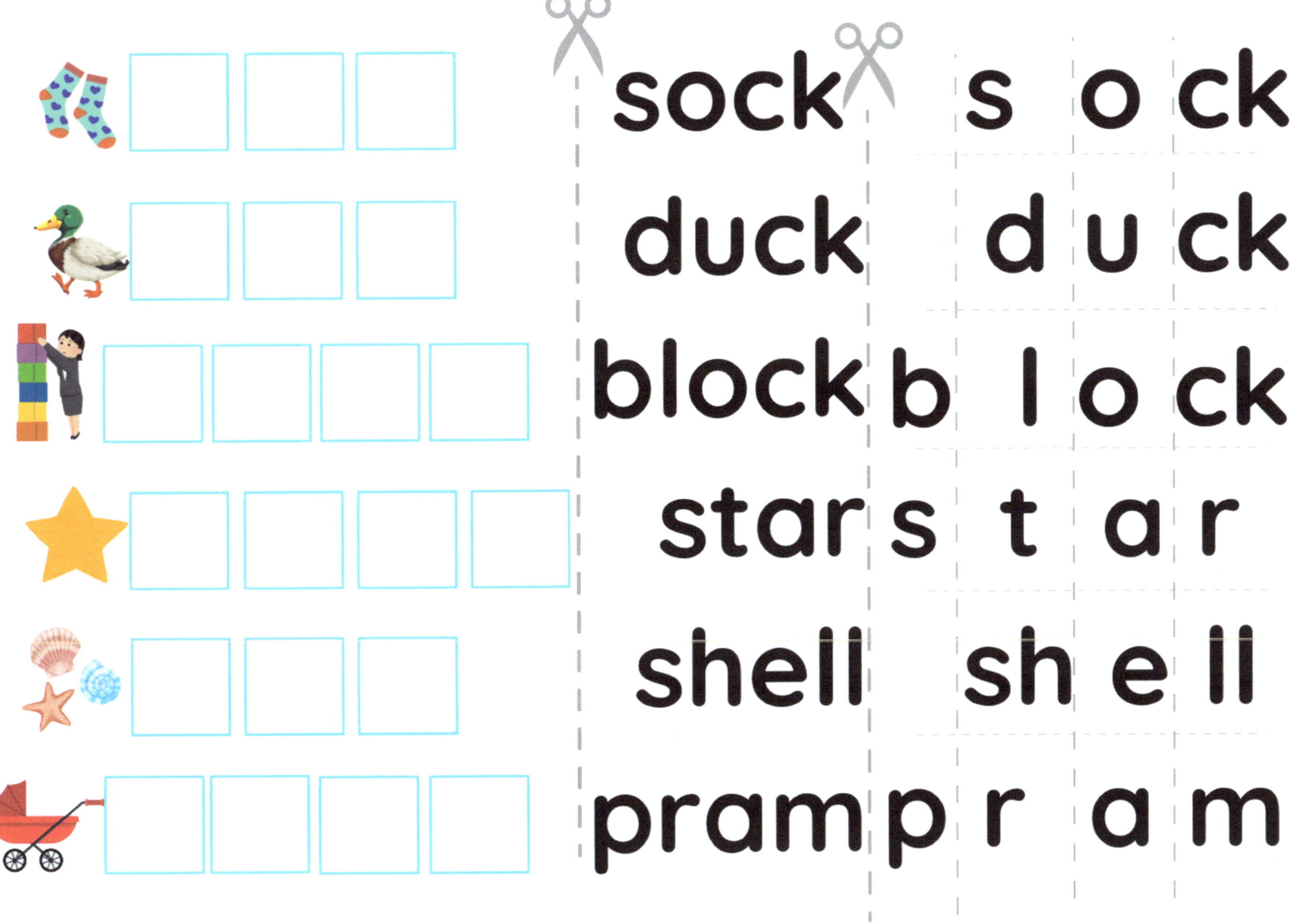

sock
s o ck
duck
d u ck
block
b l o ck
star
s t a r
shell
sh e ll
pram
p r a m

Each picture starts with one of the consonant blends below.
Connect the consonant blend with the right picture.

grapes pram blocks plant brush princess bread brain plum plane globe black

Connect the consonant blend with the right picture

train crab drum tractor class tree clock drone crown cross cloud dress

Connect the consonant blend with the right picture

chess sun sleep shells sheep cat chick chair shirt cheese

Connect the consonant blend with the right picture

Make the "th" sound with your tongue against your teeth.
Make the "ph" sound with your teeth against your lips.

th

tr

ph

wh

wheat whale tree photo tractor theatre think phone wheel thorns thumb

“th” can make a loud sound in the word “then”
or
a soft sound in the word “thin”

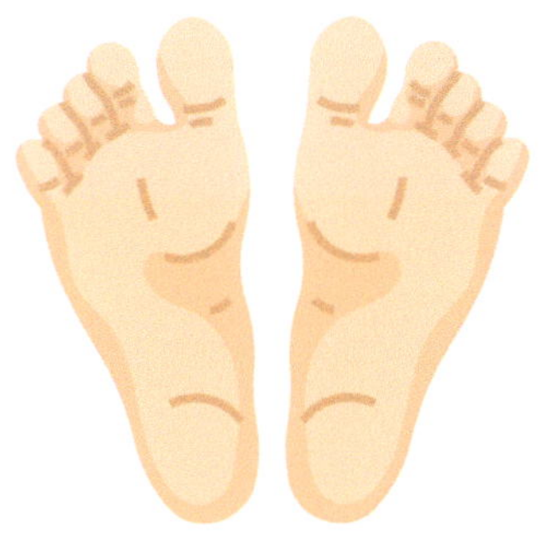

For the “th” sound the tongue goes against the teeth. For the “f” sound the teeth go on top of the bottom lip.

feet fat thin theatre fall fast thumb thorns feather think funny

Each of these words begin with th or f. Circle the correct one.

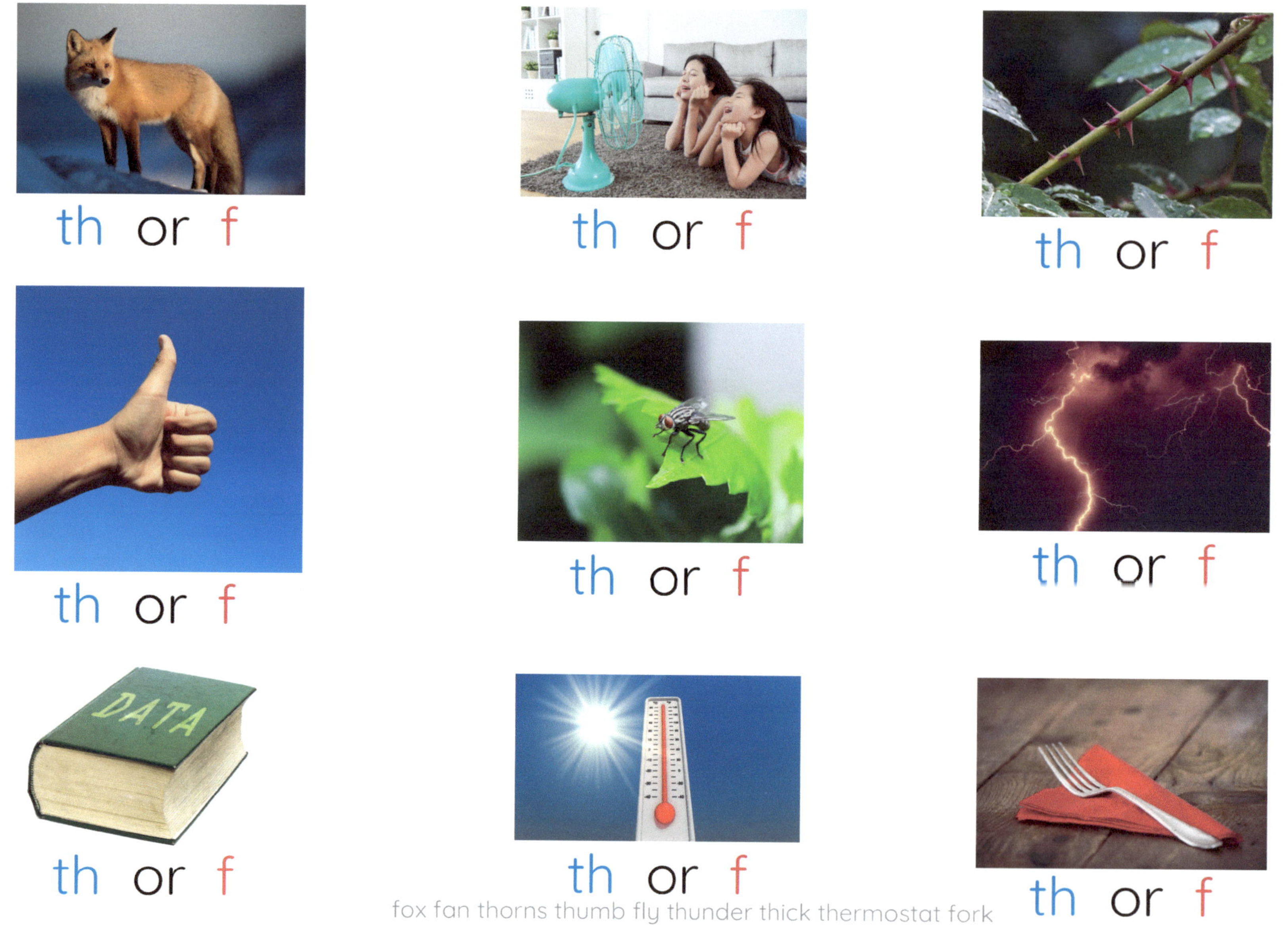

fox fan thorns thumb fly thunder thick thermostat fork

Circle the 3 letters that are in the word

a b c d e f g h i j k l m n o p q r s t u v w x y z

a b c d e f g h i j k l m n o p q r s t u v w x y z

a b c d e f g h i j k l m n o p q r s t u v w x y z

a b c d e f g h i j k ll m n o p q r s t u v w x y z

a b c d e f g h i j k ll m n o p q r s t u v w x y z

a b c d e f g h i j k l m n o p q r s t u v w x y z

a b ck d e f g h i j l m n o p q r s t u v w x y z

HINT: 1. What letter does the word start with? 2. What letter does the word end with? 3. What letter can you hear in the middle?

ink egg hat doll ball fan sick

Circle the 3 letters that are in the word

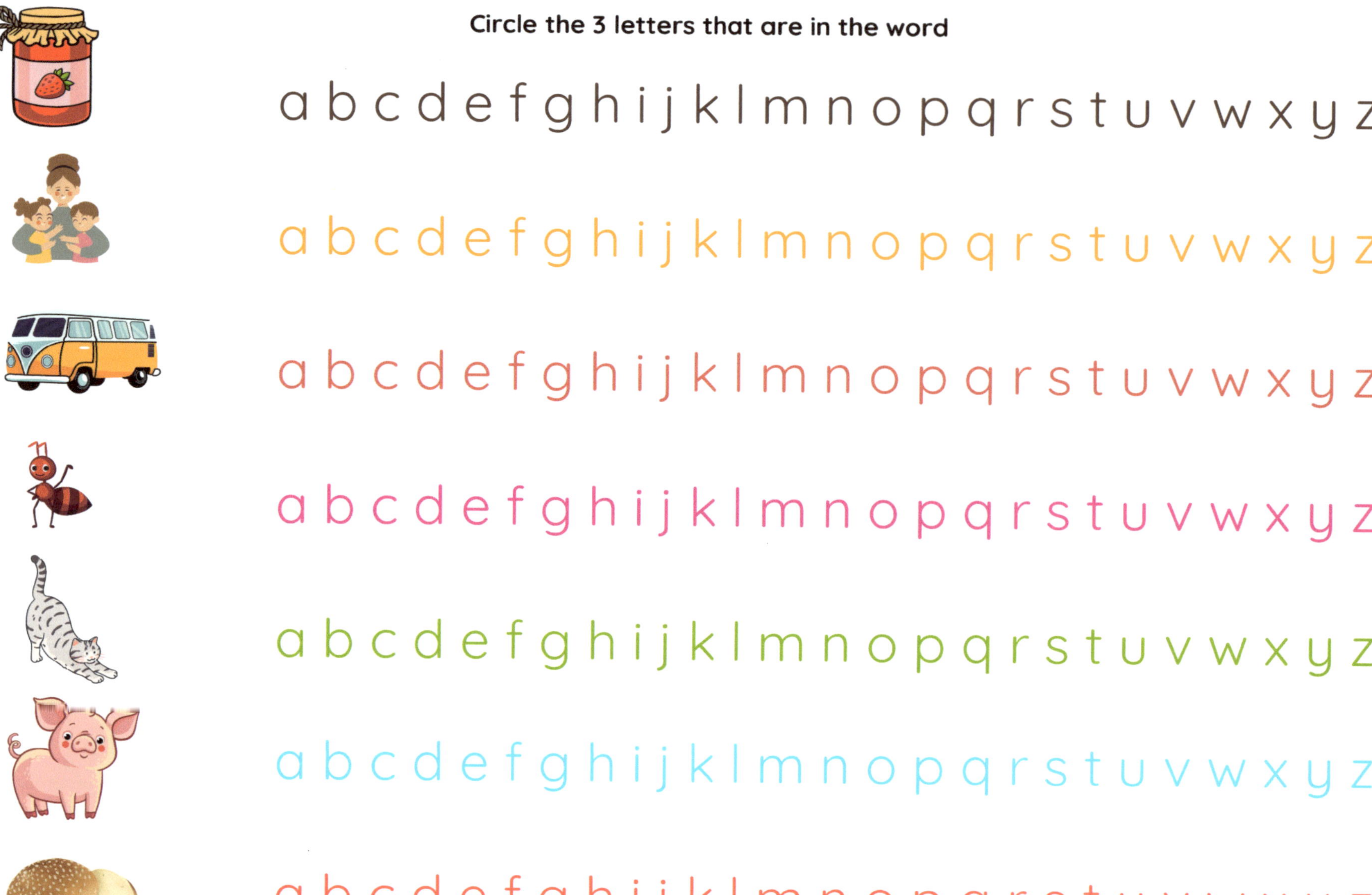

HINT: 1. What letter does the word start with? 2. What letter does the word end with? 3. What letter can you hear in the middle?

jam mum van ant cat pig bun

Circle the 3 letters that are in the word

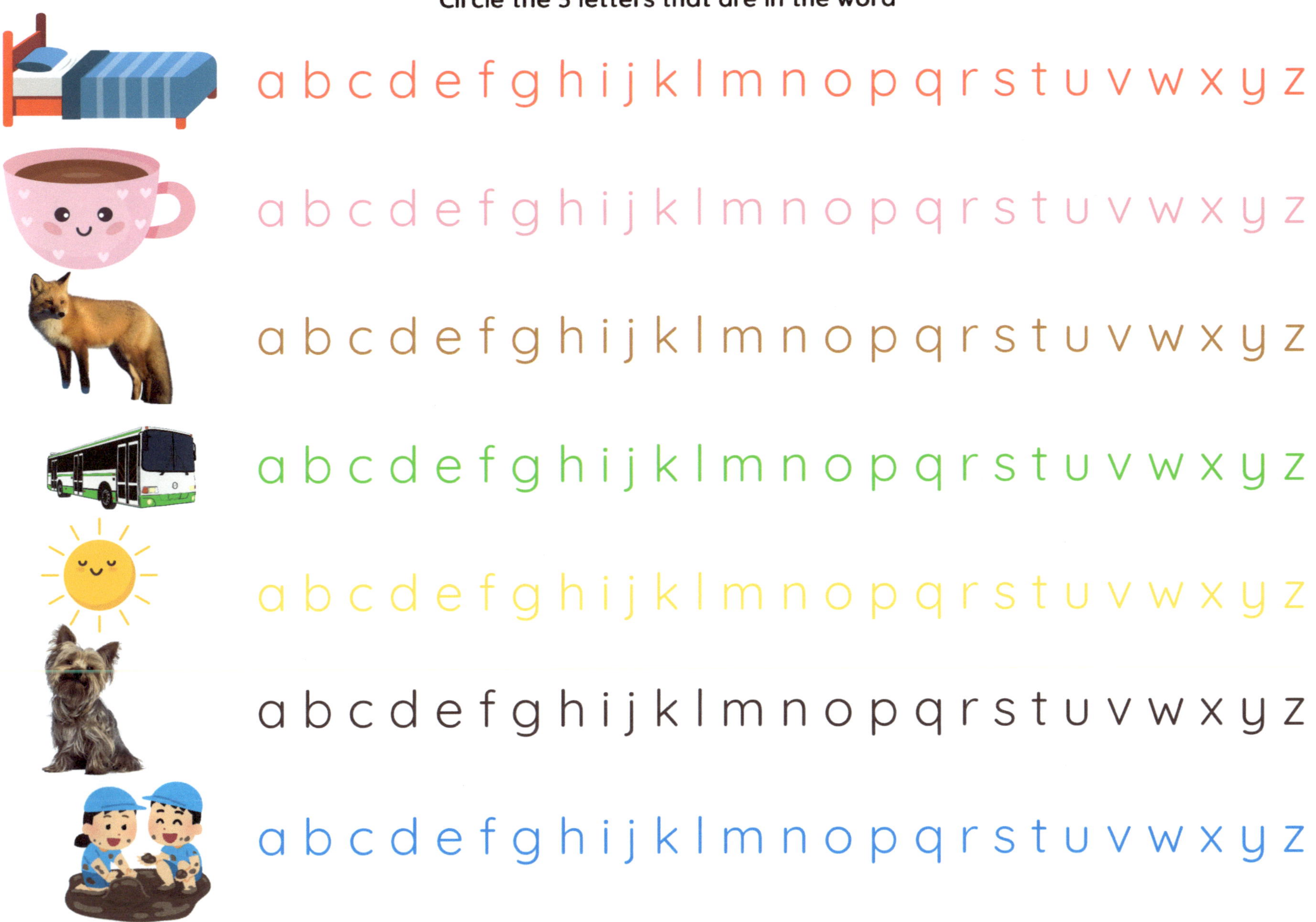

HINT: 1. What letter does the word start with? 2. What letter does the word end with? 3. What letter can you hear in the middle?

bed cup fox bus sun dog mud

Circle the 3 letters that are in the word

HINT: 1. What letter does the word start with? 2. What letter does the word end with? 3. What letter can you hear in the middle?

hug nut log cap rat bat bag

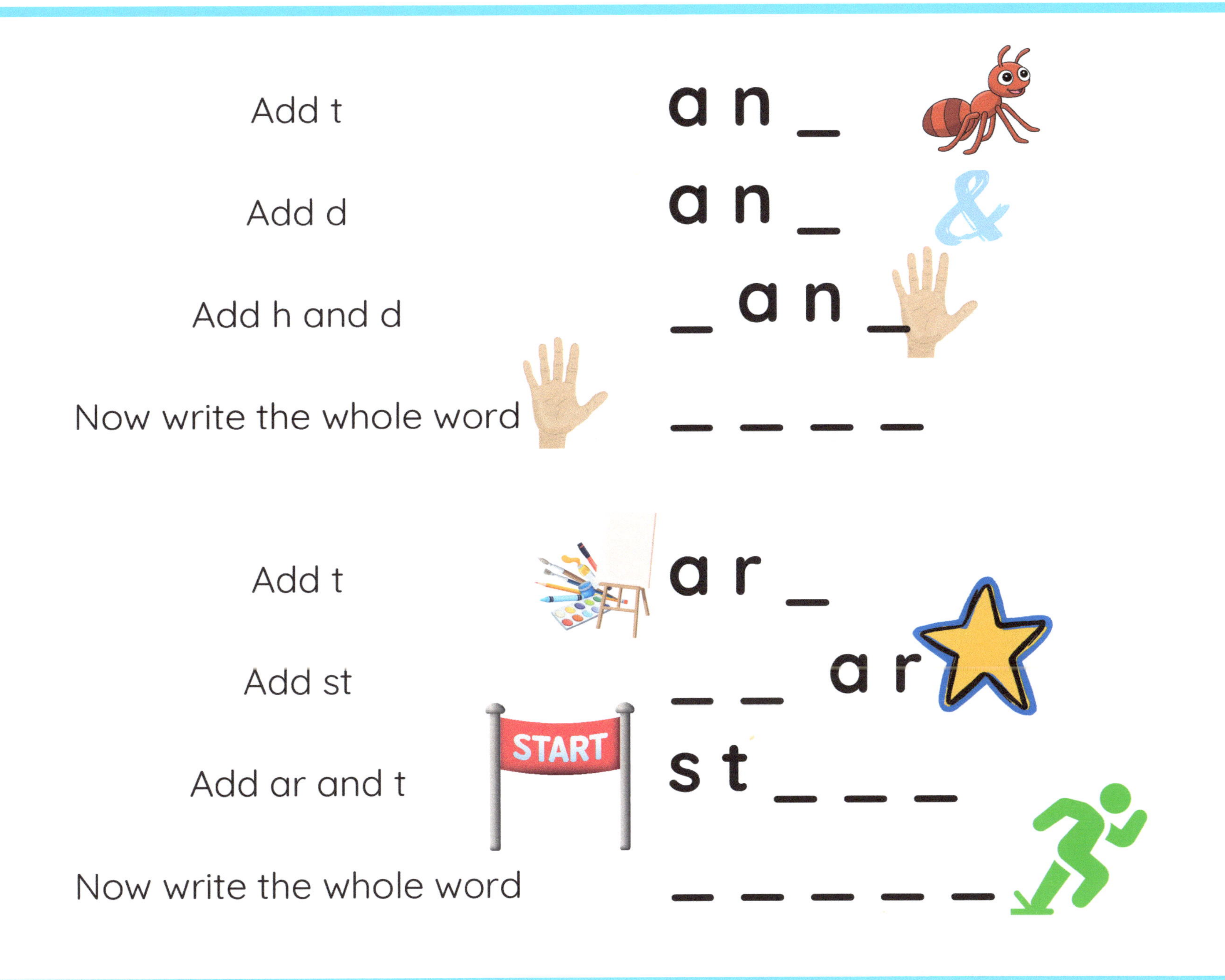

Add t
a n _
Add d
a n _
Add h and d
_ a n _
Now write the whole word
_ _ _ _
Add t
a r _
Add st
_ _ a r
START
Add ar and t
s t _ _ _
Now write the whole word
_ _ _ _ _

Add the correct letters to match the pictures.

_it

_at

_a_

_a_

_a_

_a_

_a_

_a_

s c t r n p h

_o_

_e_

_a_

_u_

_a_

_e_

_u_

_o_

t p n h j r m g ck

sit sat cat car can pan cap hat

pot hen ham gun jam men nun rock

Add the correct letter to match the pictures.

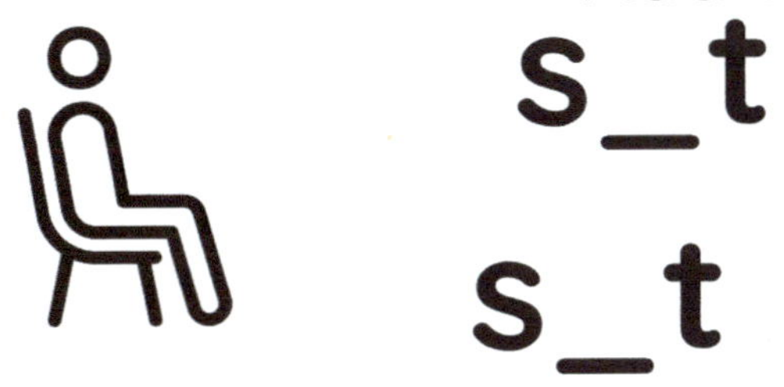

s_t

s_t

m_n

n_n

r_ck

p_n

c_p

h_n

a

i

o

e

u

p_t

c_r

h_t

c_n

h_m

g_n

j_m

c_t

sit sat men nun rock pan cap hen

pot car hat can ham gun jam cat

Write the words for these pictures.

___ ___ ___

___ ___ ___

___ ___ ___

___ ___ ___

___ ___ ___

___ ___ ___

___ ___ ___

___ ___ ___

___ ___ ___

___ ___ ___

___ ___ ___

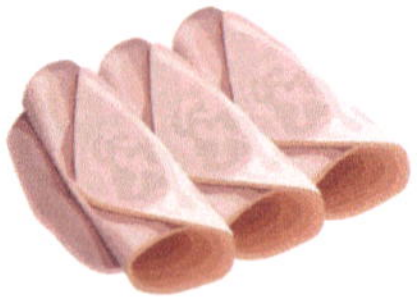

___ ___ ___

___ ___ ___

___ ___ ___

___ ___ ___

___ ___ ___

sit sat men nun rock pan cap hen

pot car hat can ham gun jam cat

Add the correct letter to match the pictures.

t_sk

l_ck

l_ps

pl_m

pr_m

pl_s

dr_m

s_ck

r_mp

b_ll

r_ts

cl_ck

gr_ss

fr_g

h_nd

sl_g

tusk lock lips plum pram plus drum sock

ramp ball rats clock grass frog hand slug

Add the correct letters to match the pictures.

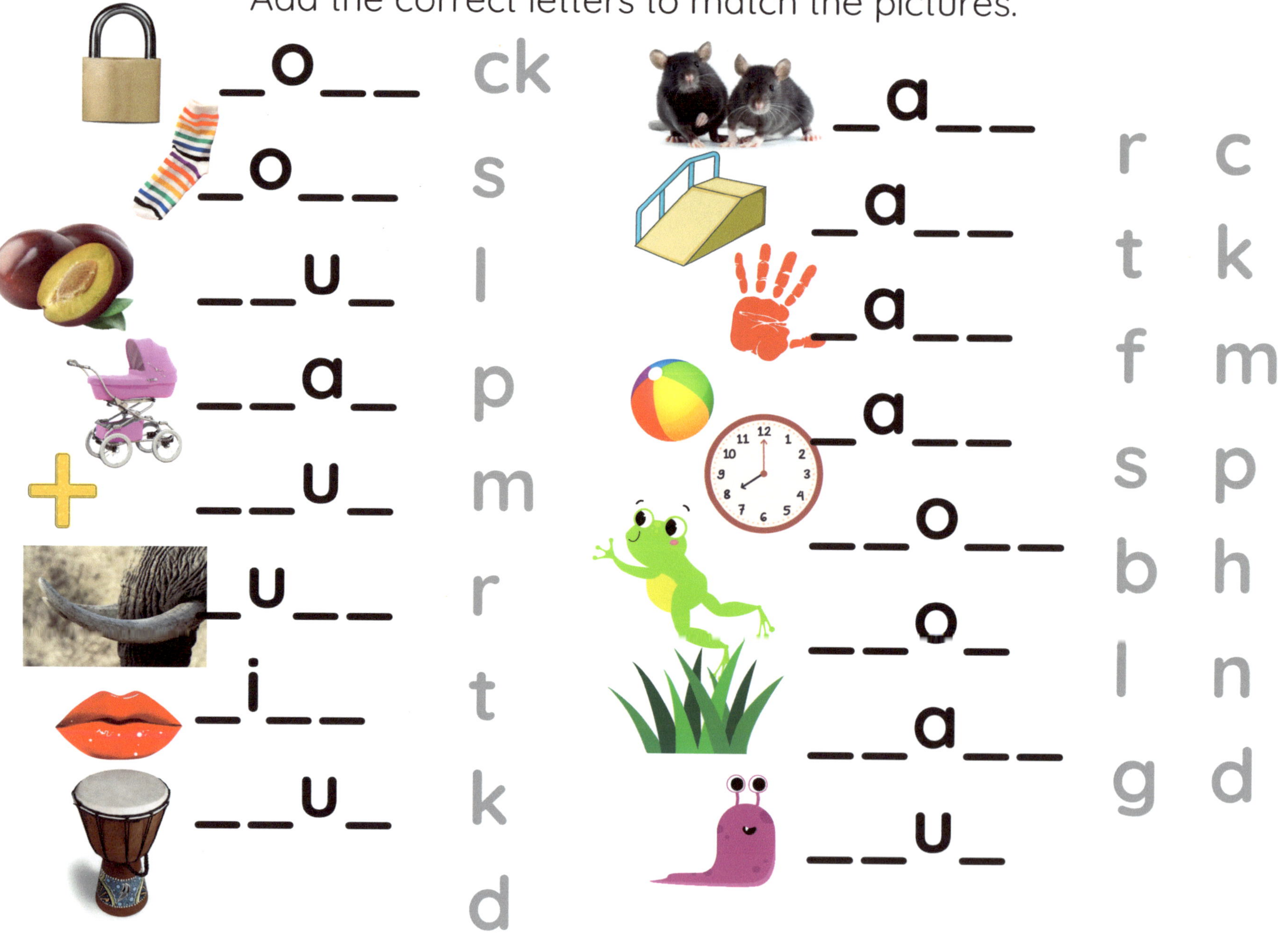

lock sock plum pram plus tusk lips drum

rats ramp hand ball clock frog grass slug

Now try and write these words.

- What does the word start and end with?
- What else can you hear at the start or end?
- Now, what about the middle?

lock sock plum pram plus tusk lips drum

rats ramp hand ball clock frog grass slug

Add the correct letters to match the pictures. Some may be a bit tricky at first.

_ _ oo _	m	_ _ a _ _
	s	
	p	
_ oo _	n	_ _ ee
	z	
_ oo	qu	_ _ a _
	ck	
	t	
_ _ i _	r	_ i _ _
	nk	
	ng	_ i _ _

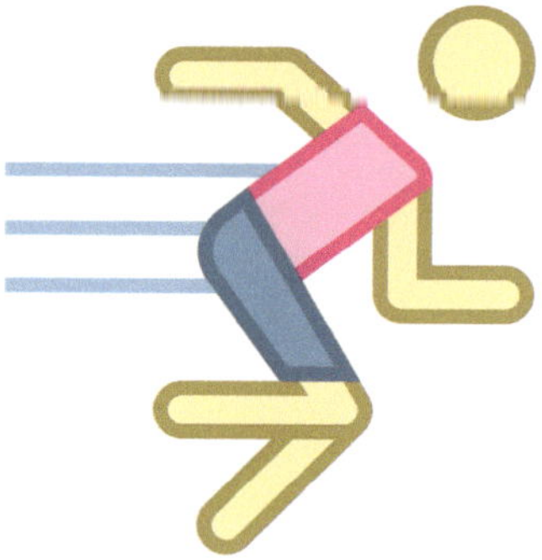

Add the correct letters to match the pictures.

_an

__umb

ta__

ri__

ch

sh

ng

nk

th

f

__ark

__op

__op

bu__

_oot

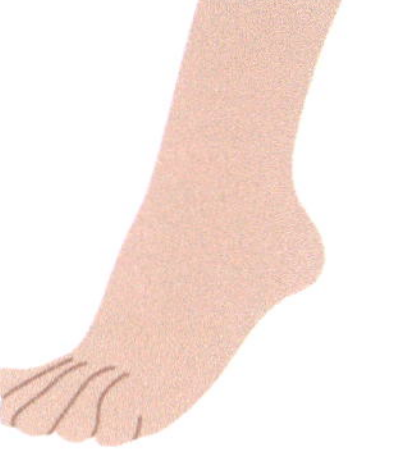

fan thum tank ring shark shop chop bunk foot

Add the correct letters to match the pictures. Some may be a bit tricky at first.

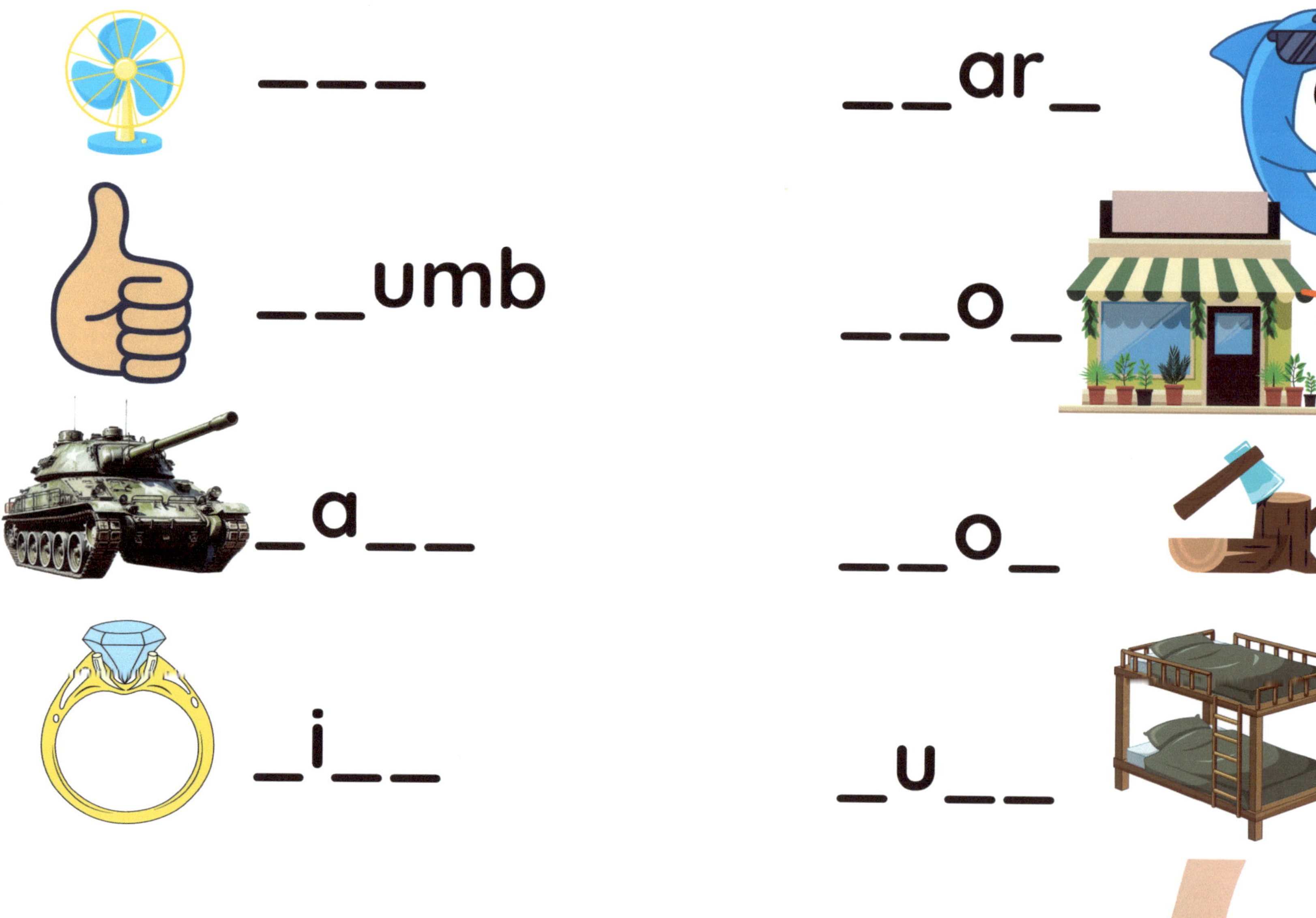

fan thum tank ring shark shop chop bunk foot

Get out your spelling book and practise writing some words!

CVC words & a few others - reading and spelling

Focus on the skill of blending cvc words. Approach the spelling of these words with questions like:

- What does the word start with?
- What does the word end with?
- And lastly, which of the 5 vowels could you hear? a e o i u

sat
cat
mat
rat
pat
tat

sit
lit
pit
pin
tin
lid

fox
box
log
dog

top
pot
not
mop

bad
bed

b d

red
pen
hen
den
ten

leg
peg
nip

bag
jam
fat

bus
bug
sun
fun
run
hug
cup

get
net
vet
yes
wet
him
big
can
nap
cap
pan

mud
mug
mum
rug
up
off
mess
kiss
fell
fill
less
bell

sock
lock
rock
kick
lick
tick

tuck
suck
luck
duck
back
sack
pack

chop
chip
chap
chin

shock
ship
shed

*Investigate "lid" and "lit".
What do you hear at the end of the word?

Copy this page as many times as you like and practise your spelling.

Example: **kick Ken**

a b c d e f g h i j k l m n o p q r s t u v w x y z

Short sound blended words

Focus on the skill of blending double consonants with a vowel in the middle of the word.
Approach the spelling of these words with questions like

- What does the word start with?
- What else can you hear at the beginning or the end?
- What does the word end with?
- And lastly, which of the 5 vowels could you hear in the middle? "a o u i e"
- We will look at the floss rule a bit later for the double ff ll ss zz.

class
glass
cross
boss
moss
toss
floss
gloss

plum
drum

flash

shell
chest

star
art
start

Ask your child to say these three words one after the other. They can often be challenging to pronounce.

flock
block
clock

crush
flush
brush
slush

smell
sheep
fish
the
then
that
them

frog
grass
step
stop
stuck
slap
trap
spill
plug
grip
slip
trip
flip
flag

First frequently-used words.

These words help us build our first sentences. They need to get comfortable with these words. It will really improve their confidence in reading and later on in writing sentences. Introduce these words by reading them first, and then then by writing them.

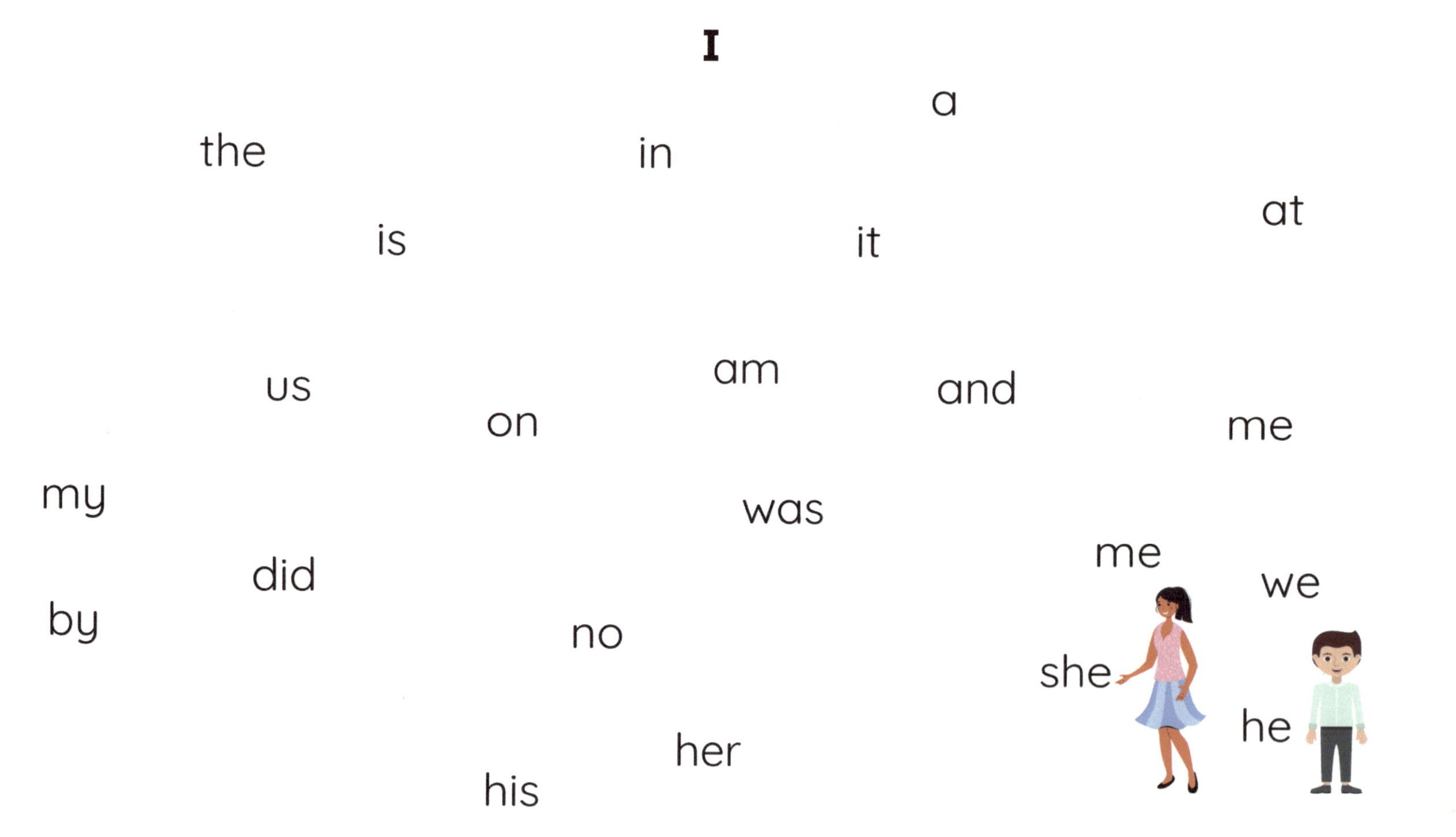

Blending - reading exercises

Blending letters has to be mastered. Practise these blends with saying the sound they make together. We start with consonant + vowel + consonant (CVC), then words beginning with double consonants and lastly ch sh th. Three letter consonant blend words are more challenging. You can do these later when the brain is more mature.

(**str**ong s**pl**ash sta**rt** sta**mp**)

man
men
moss
muck
mick

nap
nest
nip

past
pest
post
pup
pill

tell
till

cat
cot
cut
kit

dam
den
dosh
duck
dish

back
best
boss
bus
bib

fan
fell
fork
fuss
fizz

gas
got
gut

ran
run
rest
risk

Blending - reading exercises

This method has proven to support those with reading challenges. Use these sound blending exercises in preparation to a reading lesson. Especially if the child starts to guess too many words when reading, these exercises will correct that.

am ambulance
an ant
as astronaut
ap apple
al alligator
ar art

um umbrella
un underwear
im image
om omnivore

ha sa va
he se ve
ho so vo
hu su vu
hi si vi

ya za
ye ze
yo zo
yu zu
yi zi

**** Remember "a" for apple, "u" for umbrella, "i" for igloo.**

Blending - reading exercises

Read the blending sounds first and then read the words.

br brush
cr crush
dr dress
fr frog
gr grass
pr pram
tr train
spr spring
spr spree
str strong
str strap

bl blush
cl clock
fl flag
gl glass
pl plus
sl slug

2 different ways to say “th”

sk skunk
sm smug
sn sniff
st stop
sw swiss
scr scroll

ch chop
sh shop
th the
th thump

Draw a line from the picture to the matching word.

toothbrush

starfish

blackbird

moondust

butterfly

clockwork

washtub

watchdog

footprints

fisherman

handbook

ladybug

Blending - reading exercises

These words may look daunting to your child, but they can decipher all of the words with the knowledge they have gained so far. Take on a few words each day. This exercise is for reading development.

backpack	garden	chomp
camp	starfish	champ
tennis	carpark	lamp
sand	fishtank	jump
sandbox	potplant	jump + ing = jumping
crush	passport	run + ing = running
brush	broccoli	tell + ing = telling
slush	spin	sit + ing = sitting
shush	spell	crush + ing = crushing
see	spill	grasshopper
tree	spam	hammer
free	spree	better
three		stronger

Blending - reading exercises

Some letter combinations can be hard to blend .Distinguishing between a "b" and a "d" can be challenging for some. These exercises will help overcome these obstacles as well as growing their confidence. The last column contains compound words. Decipher them together at first. Read them often.

bad	chilli	sink	toothbrush
bed	broccoli	sing	lipstick
desk	lick	song	blackbird
dusk	kick	sunk	moondust
bell	click	sung	butterfly
dam	slick	singing	clockwork
pam	dricket	sling	washtub
pram	brick	slang	watchdog
blop		drink	footprints
plop	handball	drunk	fisherman
doss	football	shrunk	handbook
boss	netball	blank	bedbugs

Cover the pictures and read these words. Then have a go at writing some of these on the next page. We will look more closely at the "tch" sound in scratch, and the diphthong "ea" later.

scroll

scream

splash

spring

screen

scratch

strap

split

sprint

stretch

shrimp

shrub

Connect the consonant blend with the right picture
and then write the correct letters at the beginning of each word

scroll splash screen shrimp sprint scream spring scratch split stretch shrub

Blending - Reading Exercises

These words contain three consonant letters in the beginning of each word.

spl	**spl**ash	**spl**at	**spl**it
scr	**scr**um	**scr**een	**scr**ipt
str	**str**ess	**str**oll	**str**ip
spr	**spr**ee	**spr**ing	**spr**ung
shr	**shr**ed	**shr**ub	**shr**ine
thr	**thr**ee	**thr**ash	**thr**ow
squ	**squ**id	**squ**ash	**squ**ishy

three	**thr**ash	**str**ip
tree	**tr**ash	**tr**ip
spree	**b**ash	**dr**ip

Spelling test

1.
2.
3.
4.
5.
6.
7.
8.
9.

Spelling test

1.
2.
3.
4.
5.
6.
7.
8.
9.

shr spa spr scr str

Connect the words with the right picture "oo" spelling.

cool

tools

moon

spoon

stool

food

broom

fool

zoom

Circle the picture that matches the phrase

pig on a shelf

dog has a red flag

cat in a backpack

ten hens in the bed

fox is on the rock

  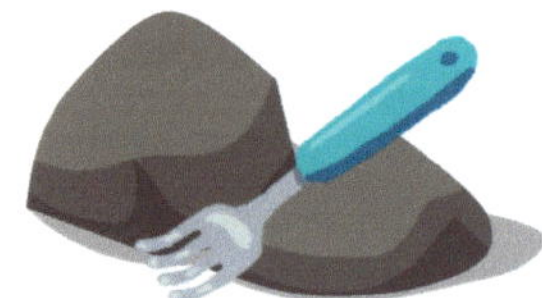

rat is in a trap

chicken kicks a chestnut

the chips and chess

 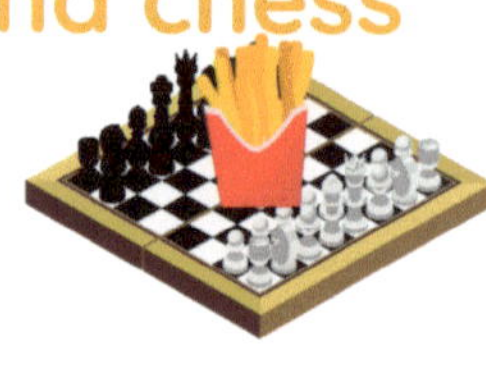

Match the picture with the correct phrase

Read these phrases daily and then try to write them.

fox in the box

dog on the log

cat in the sack

rat in the bag

hen in the pen

the pig digs

fish in the dish

chap chats and chills

Frequently-used words

Learn to read these by sight - most of these words are not spelled phonetically. This will help building confidence in reading. Start with column 1 and only move on when it is mastered, The reading scheme you follow should be in line with most of these words . Tip: Cut this page out and put it where you can see it everyday.

am	at	him	that	when	you
is	an	her	them	long	new
in	a	she	this	after	other
it	a lot	he	put	all	our
on	or	we	what	been	where
if	the	me	was	seen	why
as	will	of	to	old	are
had	get	off	do	short	were
for	with	from	so	any	come
up	did	can	no	many	saw
us	his	but	go	much	how

Cut these out and construct sentences. Start with only using a few words and build it up over time

I	They	You
and	good	tall
a	short	hat
the	We	at
go	of	in
to	is	on

live	It	food
have	She	The
love	He	forest
run	This	swim
walk	hen	pool
talk	can	garden

Cut these out and construct sentences. Start with only using a few words and build it up over time

lot	shark	watch
fun	dog	rat
park	cat	ball
swings	sit	catch
hut	mat	birds
lolly	sleeps	fish

Use the words from the previous pages and build these sentences. Once you have constructed these sentences, glue each sentence here.

You will notice that you only have one “I” to glue. Write the remaining repeating words instead.

If the child finds this extremely challenging, glue the individual words on thicker paper, and repetitively build a few sentences daily.

I walk in the garden.

I swim in the pool.

I love the food.

He is tall.

She is short.

This is a big hat.

The food is good.

They run in the forest.

The hen can talk.

I go to the pool.

It is a lot of fun at the park and on the swings.

You and I can have a lolly.

We live in a hut.

Now, read the sentence below and then write them. See how much of the sentence you can write without looking at it again.

I walk in the garden.

I swim in the pool.

I love the food.

He is tall.

She is short.

This is a big hat.

The food is good.

They run in the forest.

The hen can talk.

I go to the pool.

It is a lot of fun at the park and on the swings.

You and I can have a lolly.

We live in a hut.

Spelling test

1.

2.

3.

4.

5.

6.

7.

8.

9.

q can never be alone! Always write “q” with “u”.
Circle all the “qu” below.

qu qu qu qu qu qu qu qu qu qu qu qu

We don`t sound the “u”. Just the sound “q”

qu + i + ck = quick

qu + a + ck = quack

qu + i + t = quit

qu + e + n + ch = quench

Connect the words to the right picture.

This exercise is merely to get use to these two letters being used together. We look at this sound in more detail in the next book.

Spelling test

1.
2.
3.
4.
5.
6.
7.
8.
9.

Vowels - introduction to the next book

Vowel says its name

Letter **sounds** are different from letter **names**.
Every vowel letter can be associated with at least 2 sounds!

SHORT SOUND the SOUND a letter makes

a e o u i

in

apple egg orange umbrella insect

LONG SOUND the NAME of the letter

A E O U I

We will refer to the **name** of a letter by putting it in brackets

{A} {E} {O} {U} {I}

{A} in acorn, {E} in equip, {O} in oh no, {U} in united, {I} in icon

Circle all 5 vowels in each row. Cover the previous line when doing a new line. Practise 1-2 lines a day.

a b c d e f g h i j k l m n o p q r s t u v w x y z

a b c d e f g h i j k l m n o p q r s t u v w x y z

a b c d e f g h i j k l m n o p q r s t u v w x y z

a b c d e f g h i j k l m n o p q r s t u v w x y z

a b c d e f g h i j k l m n o p q r s t u v w x y z

a b c d e f g h i j k l m n o p q r s t u v w x y z

a b c d e f g h i j k l m n o p q r s t u v w x y z

a b c d e f g h i j k l m n o p q r s t u v w x y z

a b c d e f g h i j k l m n o p q r s t u v w x y z

a b c d e f g h i j k l m n o p q r s t u v w x y z

The "a" for apple	**-**	**says its name "A"**	acorn
The "u" for umbrella	**-**	**says its name "U"**	uniform
The "i" for igloo	**-**	**says its name "I"**	item
The "e" for egg	**-**	**says its name "E"**	email
The "o" for orange	**-**	**says its name "O"**	oh!

Practise this!!!
Refer to the ABC song here...

The "y" is our cameleon. It changes colour.
Sometimes it is a vowel like the a e i o u and other times it prefers to be a consonant.

Often the "y" helps out the "I". We will look at this in more detail in the next book.

y

Our other good helper is the "e".
The "e" comes to the rescue, when we are in a sticky situation. More of this in the next book.

Long vowel sounds in the next book

When two vowels go walking, the first one does the talking ...it says its name

a + i ai {A}
a + y ay {A}

- train
- brain
- pay
- clay

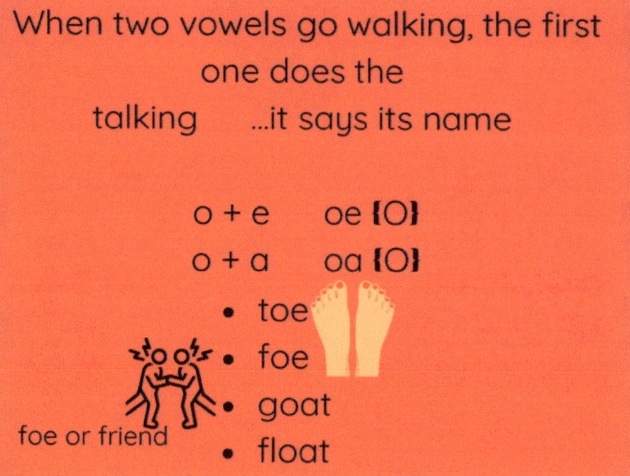

For a short vowel sound to say its name, you can add an "e" on the end of a word.

a _ e	{A}	brak	brake
e _ e	{E}	delet	delete
o _ e	{O}	brok	broke
i _ e	{I}	strik	strike
u _ e	{U}	flut	flute

When two vowels go walking, the first one does the talking ...it says its name

e + a ea {E}
e + e ee {E}
e + y ey {E}
e + i ei {E}

- team
- green
- honey
- sheik

When two vowels go walking, the first one does the talking ...it says its name

i + e ie {I}

- tie
- pie
- die

When two vowels go walking, the first one does the talking ...it says its name

u + e ue {U}
u + i ui {U}

- glue
- true
- fruit

More frequently-used words

Read a few of these words at a time and come back to them as often as needed.
These words are quite advanced for this stage but may appear in your reading books.

there
where
which
out
make
same
take
say
said

little
before
about
seldom
often
gone
said
again

find
would
should
could
groaned
yelled
prompted
murmured
know

quit
quite
quiet
quietly
queue
quickly
quench
quality

Reward Chart (stamp or colour in)
a b c d e f
g h i j k l
m n o p q r s
t u v w x y z

Spelling practise

a b c d e f g h i j k l m n o p q r s t u v w x y z

A Logical Approach to Spelling

You can contact us by email at
info@logicalapproachtolearning.com

You can follow us on Instagram logicalapproachtospelling.

www.ingramcontent.com/pod-product-compliance
Lightning Source LLC
Chambersburg PA
CBHW042027050726
47599CB00005B/822